decorating
with mini-lights

decorating
with mini-lights

40 sparkling ideas & projects
for your home & garden

MARCIANNE MILLER

LARK BOOKS

A DIVISION OF STERLING PUBLISHING CO., INC.
NEW YORK

CHRIS BRYANT
art director

SKIP WADE
stylist

KEITH WRIGHT
photographer

BARBARA ZARETSKY
cover designer

ORRIN LUNDGREN
illustrator

VERONIKA ALICE GUNTER
NATHALIE MORNU
RAIN NEWCOMB
HEATHER SMITH
editorial assistance

HANNES CHAREN
production assistance

SPECIAL PHOTOGRAPHY

Evan Bracken, pp. 75, 79, 86 and 93

Mark Turner, pp. 60, 61 and 63

VNU Syndication

Renee Frinking, pp. 100 and 101

John Dummer, p. 19

Luuk Geertsen, pp. 34 and 42

Paul Grootes, p. 108

Dolf Straatemeier, p. 33

Hans Zeegers, p. 105

To Al...
dazzling dancer,
dearest friend

CMS UPW EA

Library of Congress Cataloging-in-Publication Data

Miller, Marcianne.
    Decorating with mini-lights : 40 sparkling ideas & projects for
home & garden / by Marcianne Miller.
        p.   cm.
    Includes index.
    ISBN 1-57990-290-1 (pbk.)
    1. Lighting, Architectural and decorative. 2. Interior decoration. I. Title.

NK2115.5.L5 M55 2002
729'.28—dc21   2001038647

10 9 8 7 6 5 4 3 2 1

First Edition

Published by Lark Books, a division of Sterling Publishing Co., Inc.,
387 Park Avenue South, New York, N.Y. 10016

© 2002, Lark Books

Distributed in Canada by Sterling Publishing, c/o Canadian Manda Group,
One Atlantic Ave., Suite 105, Toronto, Ontario, Canada M6K 3E7

Distributed in the U.K. by: Guild of Master Craftsman Publications Ltd.
Castle Place, 166 High Street, Lewes, East Sussex, England, BN7 1XU
Tel: (+ 44) 1273 477374 • Fax: (+ 44) 1273 478606
Email: pubs@thegmcgroup.com • Web: www.gmcpublications.com

Distributed in Australia by Capricorn Link (Australia) Pty Ltd.,
P. O. Box 704, Windsor, NSW 2756, Australia

If you have questions or comments about this book, please contact:
Lark Books
67 Broadway
Asheville, NC 28801
(828) 236-9730

Printed in Hong Kong

ISBN 1-57990-290-1

contents

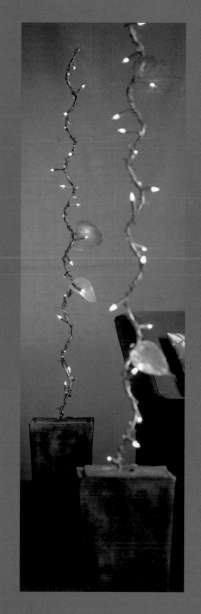

SINCE THEY WERE INTRODUCED IN THE 1970s, strands of cool, low-wattage, incandescent miniature lights—mini-lights as we call them—have revolutionized decorative lighting. Their sparkle is endlessly charming, they're inexpensive to purchase and operate, and they can be displayed anywhere. No wonder everyone loves them.

After the first brave souls took mini-lights off their Christmas trees and used them for other holidays, mini-lights quickly gained acceptance as year-round decorations. Today there is a mind-boggling selection of mini-lights, in a kaleidoscope of colors, and in all kinds of shapes—clusters, streamers, icicles, and galaxy balls, to name a few—and in premade forms for every conceivable holiday and celebration. Adding to the lights' appeal are special effects bulbs and attachments that create the illusion the lights are animated.

One important style advance is in the category of light coverings. Early mini-light shades were plastic snowmen. Today's shades come in a myriad of materials and shapes, from kitschy pink flamingos and chili peppers to sophisticated, elegant covers rivaling the best in contemporary lighting design.

In the old days, we had to have an event to warrant the effort of stringing up mini-lights. Now we know it's perfectly okay to put up lights just to please ourselves. A display is festive whether it's for the whole neighborhood or just us.

Towns everywhere are turning holiday lighting into annual community events, with blocks of houses lighting up the night with 10,000 watt extravaganzas. We love those extraordinary light displays—but that's not what our book is about. We don't use even one transformer in our projects. (Hey, we even meekly apologize for the few projects that require a ladder and a few tools!)

Decorating with Mini-Lights was the collaboration of many people, all of us coming from different perspectives, but agreeing on one focus: we wanted to share our enthusiasm about decorating with mini-lights. The lighting installations were designed and implemented by people in the Lark Books "family," spear-headed by the artistic troika of Chris Bryant, Skip Wade, and Terry Taylor, and assisted by several other talented designers.

We designed this book for people like us, who appreciate the "mini" in mini-lights: mini-effort, mini-cost, and mini-maintenance. We're always on the lookout for quick and inexpensive decorating solutions. At the same time we want them to look so fantastic that everyone is thoroughly impressed. We think we found our answer in mini-lights, and we hope you do, too.

mini-light basics

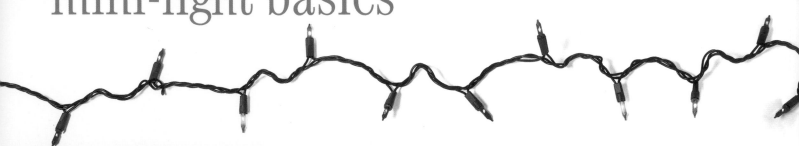

the technical stuff

If your mini-light display blows a fuse, starts a fire, trips your Aunt Edna on her way to the dessert table, or comes crashing down on your toddler—no matter how great it looks, you're not going to be happy. We put the technical and safety stuff about mini-lights up front—so you'll read it first, and get your mini-light adventures off to a brilliant start.

what's a mini-light?

There are three basic categories of lights on a string used in home decorating. The mini-lights are the tiniest; they have a low wattage (about 2 watts) and they push into their bases. Most of the projects in this book feature mini-lights. The traditional C-7s and C-9s are both screw-in bulbs; they range in wattage from 5 to 10 watts. The "C" refers to the size of the base of the bulb, with the C-7s being smaller. C-9s are generally outdoor lights.

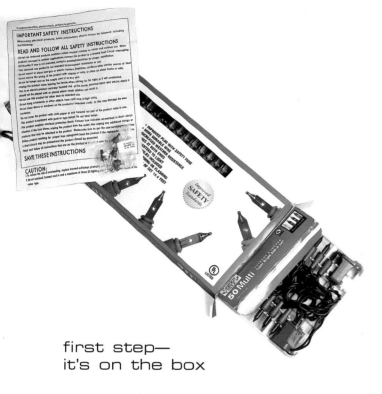

first step—
it's on the box

What lights should you choose? Where can you use them? What can you do if they're not working? Almost everything you need to know about your mini-lights is easy to find—it's printed on the box they come in.

WHAT'S INSIDE

In a new package of mini-lights you'll find the lights neatly wrapped or displayed on a plastic tray, with extra bulbs sand fuses, and usually a sheet of written instructions that augments the information printed on the package. When you remove the bulbs, do so carefully so as not to loosen the bulbs. Keep the bulbs and fuses in a place where you can find them easily. And don't throw out the instructions or the package.

ALL ABOUT THE LIGHT SET

Strands, clusters, streamers, tree wraps—whatever type of light is in the box is clearly indicated on the outside, usually with a photograph or illustration. Also indicated is the color, or colors, which can often be seen through a clear plastic "window" on the box. Since color can vary by manufacturer, you'll have a more consistent color if you string together strands from the same manufacturer.

You've got three choices about where to use your lights: indoors, outdoors, or both. Outdoor lights have extra features that make it possible for them to be used safely and efficiently outdoors. Indoor-only mini-lights shouldn't be used outdoors; they aren't sturdy enough to handle the effects of the weather.

The number of lights in pre-made forms varies according to how complicated the displays are. Simple strands range from 10 to 150 lights. The spacing of the bulbs on a cord, which can vary considerably, affects the way the lights look when they are displayed.

End-connector construction cords have a connector at both ends of the cord, which means they can connect to other cords on either end, allowing for more flexibility in decorating. Straight-line construction cords have a single-end plug.

You will see this caveat on almost all boxes: To avoid overloading your electricity circuit, never connect more than three cords together and never more than 300 lights. Don't connect mini-lights with strands of the larger C-7 or C-9 bulb. The mismatched wattages could burn out the bulbs or overload a circuit.

Heavy-duty mini-lights sets made with a thicker 20-gauge (2.00 mm) wire allow six sets to be connected end to end. Use these more expensive lights if you want a lot of lights but have few outlets.

CORDS

Cord length is listed in two ways: the total length and the lighted length. The lead is the part of the cord from the plug to the first bulb. Total length includes the lead; lighted length is from the first bulb to the last bulb. By using the cord lengths, and measuring the exact distance you want to cover with lights, you can determine precisely how many light sets you'll need to cover a specific area, and if you'll need extension cords to add to the length of the lead.

From their beginnings as tree decorations, the cords on most mini-lights are green. We preferred white cords for interior projects because we wanted to de-emphasize the cord. You might have to special order lights on white cord, so consider the extra time needed when you're planning your projects. Lights for outside shrubbery and trees come with brown cords; special occasion lights, such as those for Halloween, have black cords.

UL LISTING

The UL (Underwriters Laboratories) is a private testing firm in the U.S. that tests a representative sample of a product. If the test samples comply with the UL's set of safety standards for that product, the manufacturers announce this with a UL tag on the cords and the UL code on their packaging. Our advice: buy mini-lights only with the UL listing.

bulbs and voltage

The U.S. and Canada operate on a 120-volt electrical system. Mini-lights have a unique method of construction that allows them to accommodate the system, no matter how many bulbs are on the strand. The strands are made in a series, or circuit, and each circuit must add up to 120 volts. Basically, the more lights on a cord, the lower the voltage is for each individual bulb. It's pretty amazing. For example, on a set with only 10 lights, the bulbs are high 12-volt bulbs (10 x 12 volts = 120 volts). A 150-light cord (which is really composed of three 50-light circuits connected together) has 2.5-volt bulbs (50 x 2.5 volts = 125). Yes, in this case, each bulb is a *teeny* bit dimmer to bring the total to only 120 volts.

Do you have to remember all those numbers? No, to be happy with your mini-lights, just remember the general concept that the voltage on mini-light bulbs differs, depending on how many lights are on the set. Even though the bulbs may look exactly the same, you can't put a bulb from a 10-light set onto a 50-light set.

INTERNATIONAL CONSIDERATIONS

The 120-volt system is not standard every place on the globe. Light sets must be compatible with each country's voltage system and safety standards, which means the wire, plug, or bulb voltage can be different from U.S. style mini-lights. (The UL listing applies only to products sold in the U.S.) Countries in Europe, for example, cannot use mini-lights made for the U.S. market. European mini-light sets come with a step-down transformer attached to the cord, to reduce the voltage from 220 or 240 volts to 120 volts.

burned-out bulbs

Under normal use, a set of mini-lights should last about 2,000 hours. (Standard C-sets last about 1,000 hours.) Forget all those horror stories you heard about the early mini-lights: today when a mini-light bulb burns out, the other lights will stay lit. Here's why. Pick up a bulb and look at it. You'll notice that it contains a secondary filament or shunt that will keep the set operating if a bulb burns out. Even so, this means there is undue pressure on the remaining lights and they could burn out prematurely. Which is why we recommend you replace burned-out bulbs immediately. And also why you should keep handy the replacement bulbs that come with your mini-lights.

how to replace a bulb

The mini-lights package tells you everything. Unplug the light set. Remove the burned-out bulb/base unit from its socket by pulling it straight up. Remove the bulb from the base by straightening the wires and pulling the bulb out of the base. Insert the new bulb in the base by fitting the wires through the two holes in the bottom of the base. Then bend the wires up onto the sides of the base. Insert the completed bulb/base unit into the socket. Done! Another mini-light strand saved from the landfill!

TIP: If you're using a lot of lights in one color, buy an extra set of lights and use them as a source for replacement bulbs.

loose or missing bulbs

Things are different if a bulb is missing or loose. In that case, none of the bulbs on the strand (or series) will light and your only solution is to replace the missing bulb, or check each bulb until you find the loose one and tighten it.

The best way to save your sanity with mini-lights is avoid loose bulbs in the first place. There are a few options. Always handle mini-lights gently. Or spend a little more money for light sets with extra features, such as the stay-lit device that keeps the entire strand lit even if bulbs are loose or missing, and bulbs that have a "grip" that eliminates loose contacts with their bases.

A bulb-tester is a handy, inexpensive device that tests one bulb at a time. If you're in a hurry, bring your lights in to a store that sells a lot of mini-lights. Such stores usually have a device that can test all the lights on a strand at the same time.

how to replace a fuse

You've checked each bulb, and they're all nice and snug—but the lights still won't go on. Most likely this means the fuse in the light strand is blown—and usually that happens because, despite advice to the contrary, someone tested fate and strung too many cords end to end. Be glad all you did was blow a fuse.

Fuse replacement instructions on the package usually include nifty diagrams. (They don't tell you to work on a flat surface and in good light, so take that advice from us.) Unplug the light set. Open the fuse box by sliding over the fuse access cover in the direction indicated. Turn over the plug to empty the fuse compartment. (If that doesn't work—gently, gently, use tweezers.) Replace the fuses only with those included with the light set or of the same type (usually 3-amp fuses for mini-lights and 5-amp fuses for C-7s and C-9s). Close the fuse cover, making sure the access door slides over the top of the attachment plug and it's all nicely covered.

when a plug is damaged

The plug in a mini-light set contains a safety fuse that should not be removed. If the plug gets damaged, no matter how thrifty you want to be, don't try to replace it. Just pull out the bulbs to use as replacements and discard the strand.

where to buy mini-lights

At holiday time you can buy mini-lights just about anywhere. At other times, you'll find them at Christmas specialty stores, gift shops, home improvement and hardware stores, art-and-craft stores, and floral suppliers. Oddly, you can rarely find mini-lights at lighting stores! We couldn't find all the lights we wanted at any one store, so it seems a mini-light hunt means shopping around. When you patronize a specialty store, you know you'll see the latest products and enjoy information and services you won't get elsewhere.

Like everything else, with mini-lights you get what you pay for. The price of a strand of mini-lights varies considerably, depending on the quality, manufacturer brand name, sturdiness, guarantee, color variety, outdoor features, stay-lit capability, and extras, such as hanging clips and special effects bulbs. Mini-lights have a considerable presence on the Internet, so even if you live miles away from a specialty store, you can find lights and accessories by searching the web. (Tip: search under "holiday lights" rather than "mini-lights," and keep looking—you'll be amazed at the vast array of mini-light options available.) Like regular stores, Internet vendors offer off-season specials, so if you buy your winter lights in July, you might save a bundle.

If you buy mini-lights at tag sales, *caveat emptor*. If there's damage to the cord or the plug, the light set isn't worth anything. Tag sales are good places to find vintage bulbs, though, so do keep your eyes open for them. Antique collectors won't agree, but we think it's perfectly fine, in fact, advisable, to use the vintage bulbs in brand new cords.

safety issue #1: ELECTRICITY

Mini-lights are electrical devices. That means if they are mis-used they can blow your circuits or cause a fire. It happens. Here's how to make mini-lights as safe as the manufacturers intend them to be.

Mini-lights share the same safety precautions as all other electrical devices—don't use them if the insulation is cracked, the cords are frayed, or the plugs are squashed.

Because they're so petite, mini-lights burn cooler than bigger bulbs. But they do emanate heat, and when a lot of mini-lights are contained in a small space, it can get hot. You should never leave mini-lights on unattended. We're big fans of using a timer on mini-light displays—it's a painless way to make sure the lights go off even if you forget.

Don't overload your electrical circuits. That means read the cautions on the packages of mini-lights and don't connect more than three cords to one outlet. Your home's electricity should be able to handle the simple projects in this book. However, if you're in an older home, which has less power-bearing capability, and you get mini-light mania, you need to find out how much wattage your house can bear. You can get information from your local electricity provider.

If you're lighting outdoors, use a *ground fault circuit interrupter (GFCI)* on each circuit. (The U.S. National Electrical Code now requires them for exterior outlets.) If the current leaks

through frayed or damaged wires, the interrupter shuts it off before it can hurt anyone. You can find GFCIs at your local hardware store and install them yourself in your exterior outlets. If you're going to do extensive outdoor lighting, however, experts advise an upgrade into a GFCI breaker, which an electrician, not you, should install in the breaker panel inside your home.

safety issue #2:
PEOPLE AND PETS

In our eagerness to have the mini-lights sparkling as quickly as possible, we often forget something very basic—when people are admiring the mini-lights they aren't thinking about the cords; in fact they can trip right over the cords before they'll see them.

The cord should always be kept out of foot traffic areas, attached securely to the wall, stairs, window frames, and other areas. Don't let lights hang where they can hit people in the head, poke them in the eye, or catch on their sleeves as they walk in the door.

No matter how well-behaved your children and pets are normally, there's something about the presence of mini-lights that makes them throw caution to the wind. Which means you have to have extra doses of it.

If you have young children, put the lights far out of their reach. Keep a close eye on your children in other people's houses and places of business that have light displays.

Dogs are notorious for getting tangled up in light cords, especially at times when there's a house full of guests, ands tantalizing new scents to drive them crazy. If you have chewing puppies, all your electrical cords are at risk, so unplug everything from unsupervised areas. If you have cats, don't drape lights along or near their lurking perches or any surface from which they can leap onto the lights.

Plan and then view every light display from the perspective of the worst possible scenario. If there's even the slightest chance someone could get hurt, change your plans.

sparkling design considerations

Decorating with mini-lights is probably the easiest way to transform a wall or an entire room, as well as any place in your garden. No other decorating tool—not furniture, or paint, or plants—can accomplish as much change as quickly as they can.

Mini-lights can highlight an architectural feature that is already beautiful, camouflage something not-so-perfect, make a room looked live-in even though your furniture hasn't arrived yet, and serve as a great substitute for candles on a windy night. They make any location festive, whether it's a big party, an intimate get-together, or precious time alone. Outdoors, a mini-light display both expands the amount of garden space we can enjoy at night and extends the time we have to enjoy it.

Here are a few design tips we garnered along the mini-way.

the shortest tool list in decorating history

You don't need much. A sturdy ladder when you have to hang lights over your head. A standard homeowner's toolbox with hammer, wire cutters, pliers, tapes, tacks, scrap wire. Plastic mini-light clips to attach them to shingles and gutters. Hooks to loop the lights over. Small nails or thumbtacks to hold them. If you use nails or thumbtacks, make sure you don't pound them into the wires, but between the wires or under them.

U-pins and T-pins, standard pins used in crafts and sewing, will hold fabric and mini-lights together for the few hours you'll use the decorated tables. Florist tape holds garlands and wires together. Electrician's tape secures the cords to the floor.

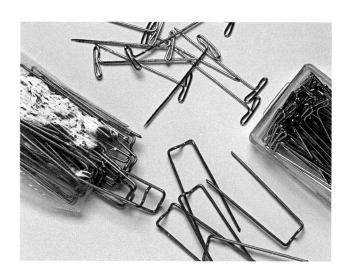

gossamer touches

Sheer fabrics, such as chiffon, net, organza, tobacco cloth, tulle, and especially lace-patterned sheers, allow the mini-lights underneath to shine through, making the lights refract like starbursts. In varying degrees, shiny fabrics reflect the lights placed on top of them. There are many shiny fabrics, such as lingerie and bridal satin, silk, and an endless supply of fabrics made with metallic foil. Although it doesn't reflect the light or allow it to shine through, velvet looks fantastic when arrayed with mini-lights.

Most fabrics are not flame retardant, so use caution when you place fabrics next to mini-lights. Keep the lights burning only for an hour or so. If it's a long event, just unplug the lights, let them cool off, and turn them on again.

shiny partners

Sometimes all you need is something to put the mini-lights into, next to, on top of, or underneath–and you have a spectacular mini-light display without having to use even a thumbtack. See the magical effects of lights in simple glass containers in Magic Embers Fireplace (page 39). Other reflective surfaces are silver, pewter, copper, bronze, aluminum, stainless steel, galvanized steel, mercury glass, milk glass, carnival glass, and crystal. Clay in the form of porcelain, bone china, and shiny tiles in bathrooms and kitchens look stunning with mini-lights. Flat mirrors and backdrops made of slivers of broken mirrors are fantastic.

mini-light shades

Shades add a beautiful extra dimension to mini-lights. They range from the cutesy plastic ones (for us it's a three-way tie between the white bunnies, the shaky skeletons, and the iridescent pickles) to delicate Japanese lantern-inspired shades in silk and other materials.

The trick to custom-designing your own mini-light shades is to make them of a material which allows the light to show through, is safe, and is still sturdy enough to last for a while. You have lots of options. We made shades out of paper, metal, vinyl tubing, chair caning, and even table tennis balls.

lights, camera, action!

Missing from the beautiful photos in this book is the exciting "action" that the mini-lights can generate, either from special bulbs or attachments. Depending on how the lights seem to move, they can calm you or make you behave like a dancing fool.

Flasher bulbs and attachments make each light on the strand flash on and off. It's easy to get this effect because the red-tipped bulb that comes with the lights is a flasher bulb. If you insert it into the first socket on the cord, all the lights will flash. (For cords with 100 lights or more, you may need to put red-tipped bulbs on both ends. See the package for instructions.)

Other effects from special bulbs or attachments make lights appear to twinkle, chase one another, fade in and out, and move in a wave—or any combination. There's even a device that can play music and coordinate the lighting effects with it. Fun!

about the projects

You'll notice that in most of our projects, the mini-lights are the star. We chose designs that brought out the inherent simple charm of the mini-lights—their ability to sparkle without being overpowering, their amiability with other shiny things, and their blithe-spirit talent of taking on numerous shapes according to how we draped, shaped, stuffed, hung, wove, trailed, or twisted them. May you have as much fun as we did!

mini-light magic indoors and out

A STAIR-STEPPING TRAIL OF LIGHTS creates a special-occasion center of attention. When the stairway is open like this one, the uplifting lights can brighten a huge area with the mere flick of a switch—what an easy way to simplify party lighting.

Reflected in the polished wood of the stairs, the shaded lights cast a warm-hearted glow. Carpeted stairs look great with unadorned lights, either clear, or in a color to complement the carpet.

Determine what length light strand you'll need by measuring the stairwell. Then start at the top of the stairs with the plug end, and drape the light strand down to the bottom. Use pushpins

starry stairway

or thumbtacks to keep the lights safely pressed against the wall so no one will trip on the lights while using the stairs.

Here's a tip from an experienced host. Attach a dimmer to the light switch that operates the mini-lights. If you want the party to sparkle, put a random on-off blinker attachment to the cord—it's amazing how uninhibited everyone gets when the lighting is unpredictable! Then, when you decide the party's over, you can discreetly remove the blinker, stand at the light switch and start slowly dimming the lights. The hint is subtle but obvious: "Thanks for coming, folks, and goodnight!"

illuminating decorative details

Beauty is in the details, they say, and this is never more true than when decorating with mini-lights. When you light up everyday objects that aren't ordinarily showcased, they glow with a grandeur that is all the more lovely for being unexpected. Here are two easy projects that prove our point.

show-off shelf

GIVE YOUR DISPLAYED TREASURES THE full attention they deserve with a string of clear mini-lights delicately trailed up and down and around them. The key to the dainty look of these lights is simple. The mini-light cords are made up of three strands. Just separate them so that you're draping only one strand of lights at a time. For full effect, make sure there are bulbs both behind the objects and peaking over the tops. We used a strand of 50 clear lights on a white cord.

Decide if you want to see lights on the wall next to the shelf. If you do, fine, just string the lights up the wall and around the shelf. If you don't want lights on the wall, then use the extension cord and light strand lead to position lights only on the shelf.

Mini-lights are terrific ways to enhance the enjoyment of your collectibles, especially when the objects are those that reflect light. Imagine how beautiful displays of silver teapots, or pewter goblets, or vintage glass of any kind would be. If you don't have treasures to show off, maybe just thinking how beautiful a collection would look lit by the sparkling mini-lights will inspire you to get started!

brilliant bar

WITH THE ADDITION OF a few mini-lights, this portable bar becomes brilliant in several ways—easy for partygoers to find, beautiful to look at, convenient to use, and effortless to keep neat. (A lighted bar also encourages guests to serve themselves, so you don't have to play bartender—you can enjoy the party.)

Mini-lights unify and embellish all the individual, ordinary elements of a bar that go unappreciated in normal light. Notice the lovely shapes of the bottles, with their colorful labels and the different translucent colors of the liquor, such as the bright red Campari. The plain glassware, stacked in a simple display, dazzles. The small bar tools are gleaming adornments on top of the reflective surface of the bar itself (a transformed medical equipment tray on wheels).

Lighting up the bar like a beacon is the glittery bowl of wine corks below it. There are many objects that look marvelous when massed together and combined with lights in a large glass container…marbles, seashells, sand dollars, pinecones, seedpods, straw balls, spools of thread, curls of ribbon…you get the idea!

You don't need liquor to have a beautiful display of party drinks. Arrange fruit punch or lemonade in pitchers of silver and glass. Add cut lemons or limes in silver bowls. For the holidays, plug in a warming tray and set out Camelot-style pewter pitchers with cider or mead. Decorate the bar with holiday drinking glasses, cinnamon sticks, and cut oranges.

star-kissed bower

BRING THE OUTDOORS IN WITH THIS plant-and-mini-light combination and feel like you're falling asleep in a cozy, star-kissed bower. Or enjoy a picnic for two on a rainy day—without leaving home.

The rooms in many older homes are small, thus limiting the placement of our newer, bigger beds. Just re-arranging the furniture and creating a simple mini-light display completely opens up this 1920s Arts and Crafts bedroom. We took the dresser away from the wall, put it behind the bed (so the drawers face out for easy access) and topped it with evergreen plants that matched the clean, straight lines of the headboard. You don't have to use a dresser, of course. Any type of platform, such as a bookcase, or just a simple shelf attached to the back of the bed, would be fine.

If you use potted plants, be sure you like their scent before you bring them home. Being so close to your face all night, the scent of the plants will be more crucial than for plants you rush past in the hallway. Some choices might be night-blooming jasmine, evening primrose, or an herbal shrub such as rosemary, which is known for its calming effects. We chose Japanese holly because we wanted a green, low-maintenance look all year. Topiary plants in various sizes in wildly colored

pots would be a charming variation. If real plants are too much work, use artificial ones: at night they look just fine, and they have the same psychological benefits as real plants.

Whatever kind of plants you use, set them out behind the bed so the array looks thick and lush. For this king-size bed, we used seven one-gallon (3.7 L) containers.

To create a starburst effect, use lots of lights. (We used two strands of 100 clear lights on green cords.) Trail the lights in a horizontal figure-eight pattern along the top and bottom of the plants. Then do a narrower pattern in the center. If you plan to turn your lights on during the day, use 300 lights connected together.

spiral ball shades

designer: DIANA LIGHT

THE THIN, TRANSLUCENT SHELLS OF table tennis balls make terrific mini-light shades. The key to success is two-fold: colors that allow the light to shine through, and a bold design suitable for a circular surface that also disguises the ball's seam and manufacturer logo. The spiral was our answer. The repetition of this fascinating symbol on the string of lights created an unexpected illusion of movement, made even more dramatic by its reflection in the shiny white tile.

You may be reluctant to use mini-lights in the bathroom because you don't want to see the reflection of the cord in a mirror. As you can see, we avoided the mirror entirely and just used typical objects you'd find in the bathroom around which to gently drape the lights. The result highlighted different textures and shapes, such as towels, pottery, plants and tile—beautiful, tiny details that ordinarily go unnoticed. We admit such a display might be a little much for everyday use—but for a party, it's marvelous.

WHAT YOU NEED

1 strand of 20 clear mini-lights

20 table tennis balls

Blue liquid food color, or egg dye

Rubber or latex gloves

Paper towels

Water to rinse the dye

Craft knife with several sizes of blades

Hot-glue gun and glue sticks

Paint pen in yellow opaque (one that marks on plastic with a quick drying base)

Mineral spirits or paint thinner

Cotton swabs

SAFETY REMINDER: Make this display in a work area with adequate ventilation.

INSTRUCTIONS

1. The balls should be clean and dry. Wearing gloves, cover the balls with undiluted blue food color or egg dye. Rub in the color with your fingers until it's even. Rest the balls on the paper towels so you don't get color on your work surface. The longer you leave on the dye, the darker the color will be. (Remember, when the light is on inside the ball, the color will appear lighter.) To get the pale shade in the photo, leave the dye on about one hour and 15 minutes. Rinse and dry the balls.

2. The size of the base of mini-lights varies by manufacturer, so check your light strand before you cut the hole in the ball. Using the craft knife, insert the blade into the middle of the manufacturer logo on the ball and twist it carefully until you have a hole that's just a bit bigger than the base of your bulb.

3. Apply a tiny dab of hot glue around the top of the bulb base and slip the bulb into the ball so the tip of the ball gets enclosed. Repeat the process for each ball until they're all attached to the light strand.

4. Plug in the lights so you can see the seams on the individual balls more easily. With the pencil, lightly draw a spiral on the ball. Draw it so you can cover up as much of the seam as possible. Beginning at the spiral's end, paint over the penciled line until the seam is covered and dry. Paint from paint pens doesn't dry very fast on plastic, so let the top half of the ball dry well before painting the second half. Paint one half of several balls, let them dry, then do the other half.

5. When the paint is dry, use the small, sharp blade of the craft knife to trim off the excess hot glue. Paint a circle to cover up any glue or any part of the logo left showing. You may need to do several coats to cover them completely. Let the paint dry between each coat.

little princess canopy

little princess canopy

IMAGINE HER DELIGHT WHEN SHE OPENS her eyes to discover this magnificent birthday surprise. Equally wonderful for doting parents is the good news of how easy it is to put this storybook scene together. The canopy is premanufactured, already attached to a ring, and draped with the right amount of mosquito netting. You can find canopies at home décor shops and on the Internet.

We suggest that the canopy lights be put on a timer so you can guarantee they are lit for only a half-hour or so every night. Or connect them to an outlet you can easily access from the doorway without disturbing the sleeping princess.

WHAT YOU NEED

Premanufactured mosquito netting canopy

Artificial flower garlands, about 8 feet long (2.4 m),
    depending on the height of the canopy

Package of twist ties

T-pins

2 strands of 100 pink mini-lights on green cord

2 strands of 50 clear mini-lights on white cord

1 strand of flower lights

Scissors

Floral tape

Extension cords

Electrical tape

Timer (optional)

1. The outside of the canopy ring should be just a few inches away from the wall, above the headboard. Measure the diameter of the canopy ring to determine where the center of the ring will be when it's hanging, and place a hook on that spot on the ceiling.

2. Measure and mark the halfway-point of the garland so you have equal amounts of flowers hanging down both sides of the mosquito net opening. Allowing for the lead on the strands of lights and factoring in the length of any needed extension cords, use floral tape to wrap the pink lights to the vine of the garland, keeping the lights in the clear, so they aren't hidden by the flowers.

3. Lay the mosquito netting on the bed to work with it. With T-pins, attach the lighted garland around the hoop and along the sides of the opening. Then add the clear lights, one strand on either side. Using the T-pins, attach both ends of the strand to the hoop and allow the rest of the strand to fall in a loose loop.

4. If you can't reach the ceiling while standing on the bed, you'll have to move the mattress and box springs aside and use a ladder to attach the canopy.

5. Depending upon where your electrical outlet is, trail the extension cord along the bed frame or the wall, taping it with electrical tape if necessary to keep it safely out of touch. The point is to arrange the cord so there's no possibility a child can slip on it while getting in and out of bed or when playing on it. (Don't forget the bevy of girl-friends who will now come over to play under the canopy. All that giggling makes them rambunctious!) And you don't want to trip while making the bed either. When you do change the bed linens, just carefully slip the canopy out of the way behind the headboard and then put it back when the bed is made up again.

6. As a final touch to the room, attach flower lights to a curtain or wall nearby the bed.

moody blue
wire trees

NOT ALL MINI-LIGHT PROJECTS ARE
happy-go-lucky. When simplicity is combined with sleek lines and subtle colors,
the result can be intriguing and dramatic,
such as these moody wire trees.

The 12-gauge (2.00 mm) wire trees can
stand upright to a length of about 3 feet
(.9 m) before they start to bend from the
weight of the strand of mini-lights. If you
want taller trees, consider using thicker
wire. Or use a floor-to-ceiling length of the
12-gauge (2.00 mm) wire, attach it to a
small hook in the ceiling and transform a
tree into a vine—who knows what kind of
jungle might result?

WHAT YOU NEED FOR ONE WIRE TREE

12-gauge (2.00 mm) solid insulated wire,
    no more than 3½ feet (1.1 m) in length
1 strand of 20 clear mini-lights
Drill (optional)
Wire cutters
Garland of metal foil stars
Several leaves painted silvery blue
Wooden box or other container

INSTRUCTIONS

1 . Choose a container with a hole in the top,
such as this box with a lid, so you can hide the design's mechanics inside it. Drill a hold in the bottom of the container, if desired, to provide access
for the cord.

2 . Lay the wire on a tabletop and tightly wrap
the mini-light strand around it. Secure it inside
the box so it will be steady. (We wrapped the wire
around a heavy rock to weight it down, and then
put it inside the box.) Do whatever works efficiently and safely to hold the wire securely in the
container's opening. (A piece of bent metal
worked for us.)

3 . Once the wire and lights are firmly attached,
shape the wire upwards. Wrap the garland of stars
loosely around the wires, cutting off any excess
when you reach the top. Tweak the lights so they
poke outward like star-seeking tendrils. Depending on how moody you feel, add one leaf or several.

good news
light shades

WHAT YOU NEED

Newspaper

Sheets of glossy white card stock, depending on number of shades

Ruler

Scissors

Compass

Pencil

Handheld paper punch

Sturdy metal clamps

1 strand of clear C-9 lights or mini-lights

Metal brads to match the color of the wire cord

Glue

YOU CAN FIND FASCINATING graphics for mini-light shades just about anywhere, as this clever newspaper shade project proves. Placing the lights inside a huge glass cylinder, instead of hanging them in a row, keeps the lights so contained they light a small area as much as a full-wattage table lamp does.

You can use the same section of newspaper for each shade just by making more copies of it, or use a variety of sections. For a personal touch, choose stories that are significant for family and friends—a wedding announcement, book review, career promotion, or the headline that declares your daughter's soccer team won the county championship again.

The photo and the instructions are for use with a C-9 bulb on a single cord. The shade would be too big for a single mini-light bulb, but it would look great if you bunched three or four lights together in a shade and let them hang down like the stamens of a flower.

INSTRUCTIONS

1 . Measure and cut the newspaper into 6 x 6-inch (15.2 cm) squares. On a photocopier, duplicate the newspapers on to sheets of the glossy white card stock.

2 . To make the shades, use figure 1 for guidance on how to measure, cut, and glue them. Using a compass, measure a circle with a radius of 6 inches (15.2 cm). Cut off a quarter section of the circle, leaving the rest of it to fold. With a pencil, draw a straight line as indicated. With a small paper punch, punch out three holes along one edge and make a small, round hole in the center. (If you're using mini-lights, you'll need to cut the hole a little bigger to accommodate the thickness of the several wires.)

3 . Fold the circle as indicated, lapping the unpunched edge over the punched edge. Glue the overlapping edges together. Use sturdy clamps to hold the edges if necessary. When the glue is completely dry, use the holes on the top layer of paper to guide you, and punch holes on the edge underneath.

4 . Remove the bulb from the base. Slip the base over the shade and insert the bulb back into the base from inside the shade. Repeat for all the shades. Then arrange the string of lights in a tall, wide glass cylinder.

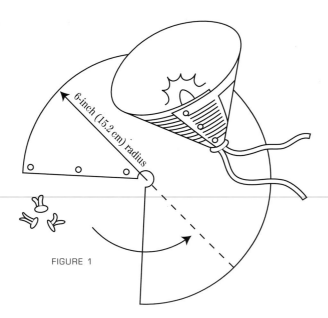

6-inch (15.2 cm) radius

FIGURE 1

Cool Fires

In a room with a fireplace, we arrange our furniture so we can face the fire and enjoy its warming aura. But for most of the year, many fireplaces are just covered up by a screen, taking away the focal point of the room and leaving us with a nagging sense that something is missing. How much more pleasurable it is to bring the hearth out of hiding and make it shine all year long.

Although we used different lighting arrays in our two fireplaces, they ended up with similar results: both offered more light than a real fire, but with no flying embers to worry about and no ashes to clean up. And nicest of all on a hot sultry night—no heat!

color glow hearth

ALL YOU DO HERE IS DRAPE LIGHTS over an arrangement in a container. In the photo is a strand of 20 vintage colored lights, size C-9 on green cord. For mini-lights, you'd need a strand of either 50 or 100 bulbs.

We used an old coal bucket we found in an antique store, but any sturdy container—such as a ceramic pot, or basket, or kindling box—would look just as terrific. Put rocks or gravel in the container to help hold the items in your arrangement and weight the whole display. To maximize the height of your fireplace, make an arrangement with several containers and use bricks under the ones in the back to give them height.

We gathered bare twigs and branches from the garden to use as our arrangement, but any natural decorations, such as pussy willows, pinecones, or potted plants would look wonderful. Artificial floral arrangements work beautifully, too. For the holidays, make arrangements with outdoor lights, plug them into outlets on the porch, and let them light the way to your door.

magic embers fireplace

A FEW HURRICANE LAMPS AND LOTS OF clear mini-lights spark excitement when they're placed together in an empty fireplace. Andirons like these wide-eyed owls allow firelight to show through, adding to the magical glow. For more reflective power, we laid a bed of white sand on the fireplace floor.

For each hurricane lamp, we used a strand of 100 clear lights on a white cord. An uneven number of lamps looks best. Vary their heights to increase the dramatic effect.

We discovered that when the screen is put back over the fireplace, as it would be when a real fire is glowing, the small mesh squares refract the mini-lights in such a way that they seem to dance like a shower of embers. Alas, the still camera can't catch this evocative effect, but do try it and see for yourself.

valentine table for two

KINDLE SOMETHING UNFORGETTABLE with this enticing table set for two. Touches of light are everywhere. There are the two vases of shiny mercury glass filled with lighted flowers. One vase would be plenty on any other day, but isn't Valentine's Day a day to be extravagant? One strand is lighted silk peach flowers and the other is white plastic. Totally different and amazingly compatible—sound like any couples you know? The light from the flowers is reflected in the crystal goblets, the silver flatware and cardholder, even the shiny white surface of the china bowl. Vintage valentines add a subtle message: "I love you for a long, long time. Forever."

One of the unexpected benefits of this type of lighting is that it provides soft uplighting, which is wonderfully flattering to your face. And, unlike candles, these lights won't blow out in the breeze if you put your table outside.

All you have to do is find beautiful vases that reflect light—silver, mercury glass, or crystal are perfect—and arrange the light strands in the vases with the cord running down the back side of the vase. Place the vases on the edge of the table so that you stare into your loved one's eyes, not the lights. The rest of the evening's magic is up to you…

glass and glittering lights

Pitchers, bowls, bottles, globes, goblets, jars, urns, lamp chimneys, vases, aquariums: glass containers of all kinds can be become vessels of light with the simple addition of a strand of mini-lights. Glass both holds the lights in one place and reflects them out like star-darts. Nothing's easier than putting glass and lights together, and nothing quite matches the dazzle of their partnership.

lights in big bottles

AS THIS CHARMING INTERIOR SHOWS, DECORATING
with mini-lights doesn't mean your other lights have to be
turned down low. This room is bright and cheery from daylight and a palette of delicate colors. The light from the
mini-lights in the bottles balances light from the candles
and the shiny ornaments and pulls the whole arrangement
together. Although large and clunky in another setting, the
big bottles fit perfectly in the ample space under the table.

There was no need to drill a hole in the bottle to hide the
cord and plugs. We just piled the lights into the bottles and
turned them on. Sometimes it's that easy!

ethereal urn with angel hair

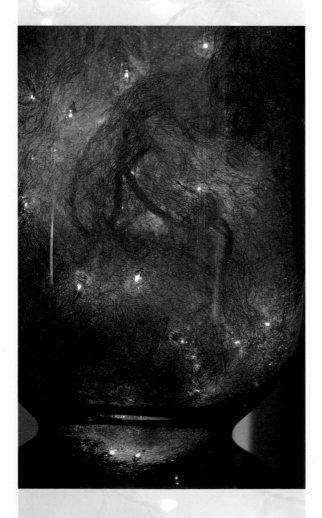

ANGEL HAIR IS A DELIGHTFUL DECORATION that reflects light in a most fantastic way. Vintage pure-white angel hair was made of spun glass and can still be found at tag sales and thrift stores. Today's angel hair is made of fine copper wire that is plated and spun, and comes in a variety of tones, such as gold, silver, champagne, and rose. Old or new, the angel hair combines with mini-lights to create a timeless, ethereal effect, especially when they're captured together in a stately glass container.

We put the urn on a column of architectural salvage and ran lights along the side of the column as if the lights were racing upward to explode in the urn. Such an arrangement makes a stunning sculpture at the end of a hallway or standing by itself against a bare wall. For the holidays it would be majestic outside the front door to welcome visitors.

We used three packages of angel hair and one strand of 100 clear lights on a white cord.

Unroll the angel hair from the package and spread it out evenly. Place the strands of lights inside half the angel hair and roll it up like a cigar. Then wrap more angel hair around that. Put the combination gently into the glass. Tug the angel hair and re-arrange it to make it look feathery and to fill all the corners of the glass container.

CAUTION: The combined heat of the minilights in one container can make the metal hot if the lights are left on for a long time. Use a timer to keep the lights on for only an hour.

sparkling windows

Window glass puts the wondrous combination of glass and lights on a grand scale, often from floor to ceiling and sometimes across the expanse of an entire wall of windows. During the day, window lights draw attention to the shape of a window and the color and texture of the fabrics that cover it. At night, the darkness outside creates a mirror effect on the glass, magnifying the lights like starbursts. During the cold months, glass storm windows double that effect, creating the impression that the lights go on forever. Here are two projects to prove how windows can be transformed with mini-lights.

window with lights and lace

LACE AND LIGHTS are the classic window-decorating duo. The window looks lovely at night when darkness shades the glass, and it's charming during the day when sunlight softens the look.

Creating a window like this couldn't be simpler. Just secure a manufactured icicle light form to the window frame using nails or thumbtacks and draw the curtains over it. That's it!

Lace curtains don't have to cost a
fortune—many laces come in wash-
able synthetic fabrics that look elegant
when made into curtains. Also the
lace doesn't have to match on every
window; in fact, you can show off a
different style of lace on each window.
If you like vintage lace (and who
doesn't?), keep your eyes open for
bargains at tag sales. Even if a piece
of old lace can no longer serve as a
tablecloth, it can take on a new life
as a curtain.

For an ultra-modern look, just use
plain sheer curtains and experiment
with lighted bulbs. Use colors that
complement one another, such as blue
lights with blue sheers. or ones that
contrast, such as pink on turquoise
sheers, or green on purple, or gold on
green—go wild!

lighted window nook

NO MATTER WHAT IS GOING ON ELSEWHERE in the house, the space encompassed by this double window becomes an elegant private nook. The simple swag lights, and the daring retro color combination—chartreuse sheers flanked by burgundy drapes—make an unmistakable personal statement: "This is me, this is my space."

Sheer fabric is so inexpensive that you can experiment endlessly with color combinations and keep the side drapes the same. Clear lights look best with two contrasting fabrics, as shown here. For a fantastic winter look try blue lights with white and blue curtain combination. Green lights with earth-toned curtains create a comfortable woodsy feel.

Although there are lovely manufactured swag light sets on the market, we decided to make our own. Here's how: First put up three sturdy hooks that are wide enough to handle three strands of lights, one on either side of the widow and one in the middle.

Using one 150-light strand, start on the upper left side and make three horizontal loops back and forth across the window. The top loop is slightly curved, the second more so, and the last loop has the largest curve. Pull all three loops up in the middle and attach them to the middle hook so the lines of lights now resemble a swag.

Straighten the curtains, pour a cup of hot lemon tea, grab that novel you've been wanting to read for ages, and shut out the world for a little bit.

merry mini-lights

Because it's so easy to make a big splash with mini-lights, decorating with them brings out the creative child in us. It's like crayoning in a coloring book without anyone around to tell you to stay inside the lines. Hang some lights here and over there. Don't like the look? Put them in a big glass container; drape them over a chair. Change to color. Change to lots of colors. Turn on the flasher! Mini-lights were made for merry-makers!

Here are some super-easy ideas to get that playful kid inside you revved up again.

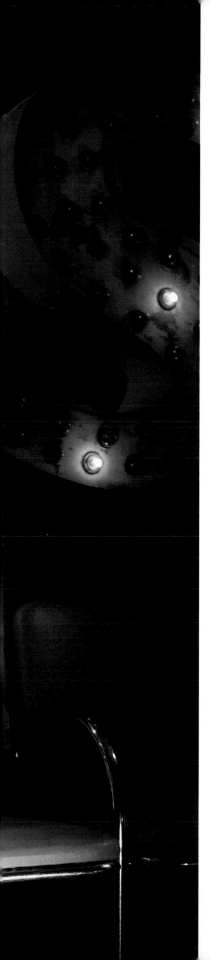

CATAPULT OUT OF THE OH-SO-ORDINARY ficus-with-mini-light phase into this totally too-fun and easy-to-maintain (hey, we even used an artificial tree!) arrangement that is perfect for a recreation area or home office. We chose a single strand of large colored balls with a pale coating that glows brilliant in the center. Team up the faux ficus with something surprising that also has a bit of light. We salvaged a giant letter from an old rooftop sign—anything gay and vibrant would be perfect—a neon sign, a display of lava lamps, an aquarium with glass fish.

too-fun ficus

You probably don't want bulbs to show on the trunk of the tree. So weave an extension cord and the lead on the strand of lights up the trunk and place the lights only in the greenery of the tree.

Be on the lookout for vintage lighting pieces. They are spectacular decorative objects in themselves and make great partners with simple mini-light decorations. They can share the billing as in our example, or take second lead, depending on how show-off the vintage lighting object is.

If you're in the right locale, consider using a giant cactus instead of a green tree. Tall, live cactus are pretty expensive. But they are hardy if you give them plenty of indirect sunlight and ignore them enough not to overwater them. With cactus, you'll need to plan out your lighting arrangement carefully because you don't want to risk getting pricked by the cactus needles, nor do you want to injure them by too much handling. Use long metal craft tweezers or salad tongs to help you place the lights without injury.

kid power central

JUST MOVED IN AND YOUR WALLS ARE BARE?
You've got a perfect canvas for fabulous mini-light displays, especially for a child's room. In less than an hour you can transform a boring room into Kid Power Central. Parental Warning: this room is rated ESBN—Extra Sleeping Bags Needed. All the kids on the block are going to want to stay overnight at your place!

For the wall itself, all we did was stick in colored dinosaur-size pushpins and string up bold color light bulbs.

With a little planning and a few more lights, you could spell out announcements such as "Happy Birthday!" or "Yeah, Eagles!" Or how about a full-size mirror surrounded by a mini-light frame, so every day your child is reminded: "You're brilliant."

galactic glow tubes

designer JEFF HAMILTON

THE GALACTIC GLOW TUBES ARE
made from flexible vinyl tubing, what you use
as a heat vent on your clothes dryer. The tubing is 4 inches wide (10.2 cm) and comes pack-
aged in 8-foot (2.4 m) lengths.

Once the project is made, you can take it
down and store it for use another time, and
being portable, it can go anywhere. The tube
can tear if it's poked, so handle it carefully.

The tubes take on an awesome appearance
in numbers (one by itself looks kind of puny),
so plan on making several. Hang them from
hooks on the wall or curtain rods. Or let them
lie on the floor, like cocooning extraterres-
trials. (Hey, we said this was fun!)

WHAT YOU NEED
TO MAKE ONE GLOW-TUBE

1 flexible 8-foot-long (2.4 m) white vinyl tube

1 set of 100 multicolor mini-lights, at least
   24 feet (7.3 m) in length

2 white plastic shower curtain rings

1 roll of white electrical tape

White extension cords (optional)

Timer (optional)

1. Attach one shower curtain ring to each end of the tube. Tug out a bit of the tube wire and wrap it around the ring. Tape the ring and wire together.

2. Stretch out and fold the strand of mini-lights into thirds. Securely tape the overlapping strands together with the electrical tape, about every 6 inches (15.2 cm).

3. From about 3 feet (.9 m) off the floor, hang or hold up one end of the tube. Insert one of the lights into the tube and continue pushing until the lights are stretching from one end to the other inside the tube. Leave enough cord length on one end to plug into an electrical outlet or an extension cord.

4. Using the white electrical tape, tape the lights at each end of the tube.

5. Keep the light cords on a timer so "Lights Out!" happens when you want it to.

pacific sun origami shades

pacific sun origami shades

PAPER LANTERNS WAVE GENTLY IN THE breeze of a far away land. Star-crossed lovers cling to one another before they must say farewell. Ah, the fantasies inspired by certain mini-light shades! These simple origami covers, enchanting whether the lights are on or off, are so easy to make, you'll want sets in many colors. If you handle the shades gently, they'll keep inspiring you for a long time.

Use a brightly colored copy paper, a translucent vellum in a jewel tone shade (we used orange and pink), or any paper sturdy enough to withstand multiple folds and translucent enough for light to shine through. Hold a sheet of paper up to a light source if you aren't sure that light will shine through it.

Measure your space to determine how many origami squares you'll need. We used 20 shades in this design and chose a strand of white cord to go with the pale shade. For dark-colored paper, green cord is fine.

WHAT YOU NEED

Vellum, 8½ inches (22 cm) square
    for each shade

1 string of 20 clear lights
    on white cord

Bamboo skewer

INSTRUCTIONS

1. Cut the paper to size and practice the fold a few times. Your fingers will become more nimble with practice. Cut as many sheets of your paper as you need. And then cut a few extra!

2. Crease the paper diagonally from corner to corner (figure 1).

3. Turn over the paper, and crease it in half (figure 2).

4. Turn over the paper again, and fold in the creases (figure 3) so the shape looks like figure 4.

5. Fold the two corners to the point (figure 4).

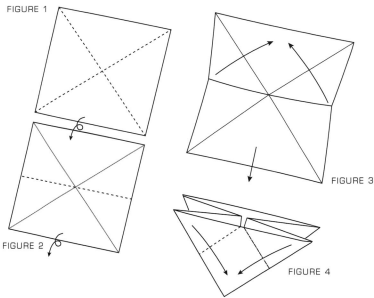

FIGURE 1

FIGURE 2

FIGURE 3

FIGURE 4

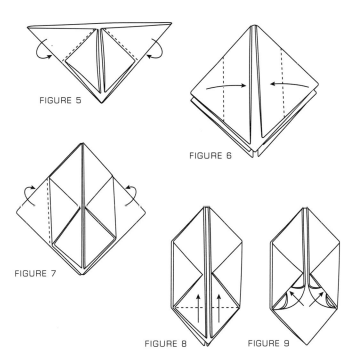

FIGURE 5

FIGURE 6

FIGURE 7

FIGURE 8

FIGURE 9

6. Turn over the paper and fold the other corners (figure 5).

7. Fold the two flaps to the center line (figure 6).

8. Turn over the paper and fold the two flaps behind (figure 7).

9. Fold the small flaps up on the line (figure 8). Then fold the flaps at an angle and tuck them into the pockets (figure 9).

10. Turn over the shape and repeat step 9 (figure 10).

11. Slide your fingers in the open sides and "open up" the shape. Put the shape to your lips and forcefully blow in the opening shown (figure 11).

12. Sometimes the shape is not as crisp as you might like. Pinch the sides to exaggerate the fold. Or insert the blunt end of a bamboo skewer in the opening to push open the shape from the inside.

13. Slip a mini-light bulb into the opening.

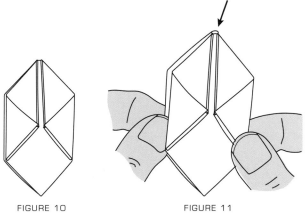

FIGURE 10

FIGURE 11

bold
metal hoops

INSTALLED ON A FENCE TO celebrate a special event in the spring, these marvelous metal hoops are so pretty you'll want to keep them up year round. All we did was hang store-bought metal wreath forms—the largest we could find—and cover them with different colored strands of lights. We ran the cords through the spaces in the wood fence boards and plugged them in, out of sight. What could be easier?

By itself the wreath is attractive, but when displayed in a group, as is the case with so many objects, its appeal is amplified. Of course, you can use smaller displays indoors. Also, it's very easy to attach decorations to these wreaths. Just use floral tape or wire, depending on the material you're attaching—evergreens, raffia, fresh flowers. Many naturals look great when partnered with metal and mini-lights. For the holidays, go all out—decorate the whole length of the fence with hoops and hang a few in the trees, too.

majestic grape arbor

AS SO MANY HOLLYWOOD FILMMAKERS know, lights reflected in wet pavement create a dramatic visual impact that nothing else seems to duplicate. You can enjoy this same drama any rainy day with mini-lights reflected on brick or stone patios.

Mini-lights accentuate the grandeur of the majestic grape arbor in the photo. The white lights trail down the columns to amplify its height. Bright magenta lights, formed in the shape of clusters of grapes, seem to capture the essence of the fruit that will honor the arbor in the summer. You can use similar techniques in your own backyard areas: go as wild and effusive as you want with the colors and shapes of mini-lights. The stones and bricks can handle it!

PHOTO ABOVE AND ON FACING PAGE © 2001 MARK TURNER

star arcs arbors

THESE BEAUTIFUL LIGHTED arbors are proof that sometimes all you need is the glory of nature and a few strands of lights to be all right with the world. During the summer, roses cover the arbors in cascades of color. Every night, regardless of the season, the mini-lights shine.

Imagine seeing the fescue grass sway in the breeze, covering and uncovering the lights, making them appear to chase one another along the arcs. Imagine creating something equally wonderful in your own garden. It's easy. To make a permanent arbor out of metal, such as the ones in the photo, you'll need some welding experience, a tall ladder, and friendly helpers. Here's how to make the simplest of arbors, one with only four arcs.

WHAT YOU NEED

Measuring tape
Makeshift compass
Posthole digger
2 lengths of mild steel bar stock,
    ½-inch (1.3 cm) diameter, 20 feet (6.1 m) in length
Stepladder
Gravel, as needed
Welding equipment
Wire

INSTRUCTIONS

Select a flat site. Remove brush and debris and rake it smooth. With the tape measure, measure on the ground the radius of the arbor you want.

To make a makeshift compass, first drive a stake into what will be the center of the circle. Attach a length of string that reaches to the perimeter and tie a sharp stick on that end. Stretch out the string and with the sharpened stick at the end, mark out a circle.

While they are still on the ground, bend the two steel bars into half-circles. Use a posthole digger to dig four 24-inch-deep (60.9 cm) holes at four equidistant spots on the circle. With your helpers, insert the four ends of the two bars into opposite holes on the circle. With your helpers holding the bars steady, set up your step ladder and welding equipment in the center. Weld the four arcs of the bars together where they intersect at the top.

Backfill the holes with gravel and soil to hold the bars securely. Use wire to tie on the mini-lights. Cluster the lights at the top if you are just using lights. If you're going to add climbing plants, make a single trail of lights along the arcs.

If you don't want to make a permanent arbor, use the same principles to make a tipi-shaped arbor out of bamboo poles. Instead of welding, tie the poles together at the top with wire. Whatever material you use to make your lighted arbor, it will look spectacular every night of the year.

63

twinkling trellis trio

MAKE FESTIVE TEMPORARY garden accents with this display of store-bought pyramid trellises. All we did was string strands of multi-colored lights on trellises of different heights. We didn't even have to choose which three colors. Many light strands already come with a selection of three colors, and often they are much cleverer combinations than we might have thought of ourselves. To keep the sharp definition of the pyramid shape, we put the lights just along the sides and bottom of the structures and loosely draped them on the ground below.

As a garden accent, the trellises look best if they're placed in a spot with plants of varying heights. Put the trellises to work—as welcoming beacons to help your guests find their way to your house, or guide them to designated areas, such as the jacuzzi or barbecue.

Imagine how charming these trellises would be if a climbing vine such as moon-flower, which blooms at night, were also trailed up its side. By planning ahead, you can get your plants and lights coordinated so they are both in bloom on the night of your big summer party. For a wonderland effect in winter gardens, drape the trellises with gold and snow-white lights. Simple displays such as these trellises also look fantastic indoors, any season of the year.

four seasons of festive mini-lights

romantic spring

Emerging from the long, cold nights of winter, spring enters tentatively, sidestepping rain showers and breezes that range from gentle to downright pushy. Mini-lights for spring events accentuate the Easter egg pastels—pale yellow, robin's egg blue, rosebud pink—everything sparkles, but shyly. We dreamed up a fresh flower wedding and a few other projects that could go with it. (Of course, what's wonderful for spring mini-lights is good for the rest of the year, too!)

glowing
spring wedding
arbor

designer **JOSENA AIELLO-BADER**

WITH VISIONS OF FAIRY
tale weddings dancing through our
heads, we gathered fresh flowers and
a galaxy of twinkling lights to make
a wedding arbor today's couple will
remember forever. It takes time to
decorate an arbor, but it's easy once
you get the feel of it, and the end result is exquisitely satisfying. It just
seems to be one of those things in life
that you ought to do at least once.

CHOOSING AN ARBOR

Arbors have become so popular that you'll have no
trouble purchasing one from a garden shop or catalog,
craft store, home improvement store, or one of dozens
of sites on the Internet. (You can even rent them from
florists and wedding planners.) They range considerably
in price, depending on what they're made of, and how
complex the design is.

A large wooden arbor, meant to withstand the vagaries
of the elements, needs to have a safe permanent installation—a process that takes time—so if you want to
keep the arbor up after the big day, then plan accordingly. Small, lightweight arbors, such as the metal
tubing arches sold in craft stores, are quite portable
and can be set up quickly. Remember though, winds do
blow, even on wedding days, so always consider safety
(and the price of the bride's wedding dress caught in a
flying arbor!) and securely install the arbor.

LIGHTING THE ARBOR

Choose a safe, flat, visually attractive location for the
arbor, one that will provide all the guests a view of the
ceremony. Determine how much cord you'll need for
both the lights and the extension cords and check
everything out to make sure it's working. Do yourself
(and the nervous bride) a favor and have extra lights
and extension cords available, just in case.

Hang the lights to accentuate the structural lines of the
arbor. Basically you'll want to have more lights on the
top than on the sides to give the arbor height and create the impression the couple is standing under a
canopy of cascading stars. Here's how we decorated our
heavy, square-topped arbor. Adjust the steps accordingly
for your own arbor.

4 strands of 150 clear lights, for a total of 600

1 set of hedge lights

2 strands of 50 clear lights, if needed,
   for a total of 100

Ladder

Thumbtacks

Hammer, if needed

INSTRUCTIONS

1. Decorate the arbor one side at a time. Run the extension cord and plug end of the light strand up the backside of the arbor so the lights start at the top of the arbor. Keep the lights on while you work so you can see what you're doing.

   Start at the front of the arbor, hang the light strand down a few feet and loop it back to the top. The goal is to make the lights on the top look as if they are vines or icicles hanging down, each one of a different length.

2. Move over 8 inches (20 cm) or so toward the side, and hang down the next section of lights, only don't hang this one as far as the first section. Hang the next icicle at a slightly different length. Repeat this process until the rear of the arbor has lights hanging down about as far as the front does.

3. Do the same thing on the other side, so the two sides are similar. Stand back, look at the arbor, and make adjustments, if needed.

4. Place the hedge lights over the top of the arbor and let them hang down. This will provide enough lighting for reading vows and placing the rings. Plug it in and make adjustments as necessary.

ADDING THE GREENERY

At night, a lighted arbor decorated with artificial flowers can look perfectly lovely. You can find garlands of all kinds of flowers and greenery in craft stores and choose them according to the season of the year. For a wedding, however, you'll probably want the special touch and loving message of real plants. You can buy all your flowers from a florist (reliable, but expensive), grow your own (would you have enough time?), make all your friends give you flowers from their gardens (fun, but can you get everyone coordinated?) or do what we did: with help from a few gentle friends and children, gather them yourself with permission from friendly neighbors the night before the wedding.

For this arbor we gathered five plants: ivy, and four flowers, including honeysuckle and Japanese dogwood. Flower gathering is not an exact science—we picked enough flowers to match the size of a person, a bundle about 5½ feet (1.7 m) long and 2½ feet (.7 m) around. You can never have too many flowers. If you don't use them all in the arbor, you'll use them to decorate other places in the wedding.

INSTRUCTIONS

1. Gently wash all the flowers and ivy to get off the dirt and tiny critters, and clip the ends. Divide the plants into two basic piles: long branches and shorter branches.

2. For an arbor this size, you'll need 8 to 10 small oasis holders that you can buy from florists. Soak them in water until they are thoroughly wet. Hang the oasis holders back to back in each of the four corners of the arbor over your head, both inside and outside the arbor. Tie them on with large pipe cleaners.

3. Place a long branch of ivy in each holder and weave it through the branches of the arbor, starting at the sides and working your way up. Stick a shorter length of ivy next to it. Do this on each oasis holder, inside and outside of the arbor. Keep the ivy close to the arbor to create a carpet of greenery and to give it dimension.

4. Continue the process all over the sides and finish on top. When you think you're finished, stand back and look. If the ivy is too long on one or two of the corners, shorten it by cutting the end in the holder and re-insert it.

5. Then repeat the process with each flower, using shorter and shorter pieces until the last ones seem to grow straight out of the arbor, as if it were a living thing. If you want to use roses, either store-bought or garden, put them in last to show them off.

6. When you are finished with the flowers, stand back and look again. If you feel you need more flowers, add them at this time. If you want more lights, use the smaller strands and fill in the spaces from the top.

wedding gift table

WITH EVERYTHING ELSE TO DO FOR A WEDDING, YOU WANT DECORATING the gift table to be as simple as possible and still look as if you spent all day on it. That's possible—the key is to have a plan and a few tricks.

We used a 36-inch (91 cm) round table.
Modify the instructions for your own table.

WHAT YOU NEED

Pale yellow tablecloth to fit the table

2 yards (1.8 m) of white cotton, 60 inches (1.5 m) wide

2 yards (1.8 m) of pale yellow sheer fabric, 60 inches (1.5 m) wide

2 yards (1.8 m) of sheer white tulle, cut to 40 inches (1 m) wide

1 strand of 150 clear lights on white cord

1 strand of gold or white lights on white cord

Fresh or artificial flowers and greens to match the wedding colors

T-pins

INSTRUCTIONS

1. Put the yellow tablecloth on the table.

2. With T-pins, attach the white cotton to the rim of the tabletop to make a skirt around the side of the table. Fold and pin it so it just brushes the ground.

3. To make the lighted skirt, lay out the pale yellow sheer fabric on a clean, flat surface (or grass that you've checked thoroughly to make sure it's clean). Place the strip of clear lights lengthwise down the center of the fabric. Then just fold up the fabric so the lights lie in the fold, and tack both edges of the fabric to the rim of the table. The lights simply rest in the fold, which now will be touching the ground.

4. To make the lighted garland, lay out the white tulle and place the strand of gold lights in it, then roll them up together like a loose cigar, leaving the plug end hanging loose. Start at the back of the table and work your way around. Gather the garland and give it a few twists every 2 feet (61 cm) or so to make it look nicely bunched, and tack it onto the table with T-pins. We made the garland on this table wider and fuller than the Dazzling Dessert Table on page 102. It won't have as many people brushing up against it as the dessert table, and thus it can hold its fluff easier. Also there's no need to build pedestals the way we did on the dessert table. The different sizes and colors of gift boxes create a beautiful design in themselves.

5. Arrange flowers and the gift boxes on the tabletop. Add a pretty container to hold money envelopes.

6. You can also make a similar table where people can sign the guest book.

white
flower wreath

designer JOSENA AIELLO-BADER

DRIED BABY'S BREATH FLOWERS, grapevines, and mini-lights—it takes only three items to make this exquisite white wreath. Placed on a glass door or window at night, the reflections in the glass make the wreath gleam as if it's been dusted by fairy wings.

Thanks to lights with battery packs, you can hang wreaths and other lighted arrangements anywhere without worrying about the cord showing. For smaller arrangements, of if you want the lights to be less prominent, use "twiggy" lights, which are micro mini-lights that stick out on "branches" on a cord.

You can find dried baby's breath flowers at florist suppliers or grow the tiny perennials yourself. (To get the fluffy, cloud-like effect of the wreath, we used flowers that had been bleached white.) Baby's breath can last as long as a year, so you can make this wreath way ahead of time and store it until needed. It is fragile, so protect it with layers of tissue paper.

Even though it's a small wreath, you'll need a lot of flowers to completely cover it. We used enough flowers to fill a pillowcase, about three bunches, 18 to 24 inches (46 to 61 cm) tall and about as big around as a quarter at the stem ends. Clear lights emphasize the wreath's classic simplicity, making it perfect for weddings or the winter holidays. Colors such as rose pink and pale blue would be equally lovely.

WHAT YOU NEED

3 strands of battery-operated lights, 10 each, for a total of 30

Batteries, 2 C-size for each battery pack, for a total of 6

Dried baby's breath flowers, enough to fill a pillowcase

18-inch-wide (45.7 cm) grapevine wreath

Hot-glue gun and glue sticks

Large chenille stems

18 inches (45.7 cm) of wide ribbon

INSTRUCTIONS

1. As shown on page 74, secure the battery packs to the back of the wreath as inconspicuously as possible, tucking them in between the vines or using wire to tie them on.

4. Each branch of baby's breath has lots of unnecessary stem, so just discard it. Break the stems only at the joints, group the flower heads together, bundle a small cluster in your fingers, and trim off the stems 1 to 2 inches (2.5 to 5 cm) below the flower heads. Squirt hot glue on the bottom of the stems. Lay the bundles on the wreath where the stem ends (now covered in hot glue) can rest on the grapevine.

5. Make another bundle and hot glue it to the grapevine next to the first bundle. Each new row of bundles should cover the hot-glue puddle on the row before it, so that each row's bundles cover up the mechanics of the wreath as it grows fluffier and fuller and softer looking.

6. Continue until the wreath is completely covered. Take your time. Working with little flowers takes a lot of patience.

7. When you're finished adding the flowers, bend the chenille stems through the vines on the top of the back side and use it to hang the wreath. (You can add a simple ribbon, as we did, if you wish.)

8. Hang the wreath, and stand back and look at it from the front and sides. Fill in any spots that still need flowers.

9. Each time you light the wreath, rather than reaching behind it and fumbling for the battery pack, turn the whole wreath around to see the switches. Then gently turn it face out.

2. Weave the mini-lights through the wreath, keeping all the bulbs facing out front, inside the center circle, or on its outside, and not sticking out the back toward the window. Bulbs on the perimeters of the wreath will reflect more on the window glass behind it; the ones on the front of the wreath light it and make it glow. Use hot glue (at the low temperature) if you want to be extra-sure the lights will stay in place.

3. Make and glue bundles of baby's breath to the wreath. Work in rows, starting from the center and moving toward the outside. The bundles don't have to be perfectly spaced, but you want to keep them full to cover up the grapevine and the light strands.

stamped vellum
light shades

designer NICOLE TUGGLE

TRANSLUCENT VELLUM MAKES THE perfect mini-light shade. It's weighty enough to hold a folded shape but sheer enough to let the soft light shine through. Hanging from a deck railing on a warm spring night, the sophisticated shades glow as if they've each captured a hundred fireflies. To enjoy the shades as long as possible, protect them from rain and heavy dew.

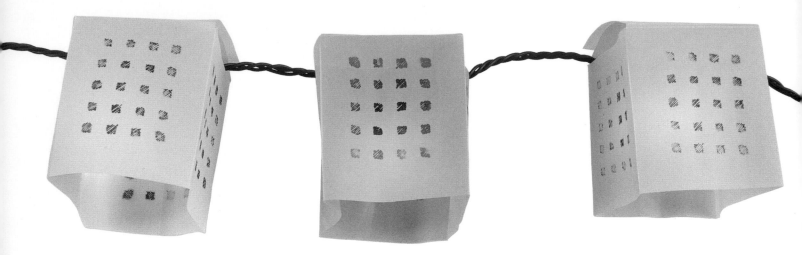

WHAT YOU NEED

1 strand of 50 clear mini-lights

1 sheet of card stock or stiff paper,
  8½ x 10 inches (21.6 cm x 26.7 cm)

25 sheets of vellum, each 8½ x 10 inches
  (21.6 cm x 26.7 cm)

Pencil

Template, on this page

Ruler

Scissors

Craft knife

Butter knife or bone folder

Rubber stamp

Black ink pad

White craft glue or glue stick

Medium-size paintbrush

Transparent tape

INSTRUCTIONS

1. Use the template below to create a template
on your 8½ x 10-inch (21.6 cm x 26.7 cm) sheet of
card stock. Outline the shape, and copy the dotted
lines onto the template using a pen or pencil. Use
a ruler for accuracy, and use the template to create all the shades.

2. Place the template on a sheet of vellum. Transfer the outline of the template to your vellum by tracing it with a pencil. Cut along the edges of your template with scissors or a craft knife.

3. Using the butter knife or bone folder, score your vellum sheet along the dotted guidelines copied from the template.

4. Continue steps 1 through 3 for all remaining sheets of vellum until you have cut, scored, and unfolded 25 shades.

5. Ink your rubber stamp well, and press it onto all four side panels of the shades. Allow the ink to dry for approximately 30 minutes.

6. Once the ink has dried, begin folding each shade along the edges until you have a rectangular box shape. There will be a small flap at the side. Overlap this flap with the joining edge (the larger flap should be on top) and glue down (see figure 1). Because vellum is transparent, be sure to use only a thin layer of glue so it won't show through (using a glue stick helps avoid this problem). Let the glue set for 30 minutes.

7. Thread the shades onto a strand of lights, placing one over every other light bulb. Gently tuck each bulb under the flaps, allowing it to hang centered in the shade. Tape the top edge shut with transparent tape. Repeat with the remaining shades.

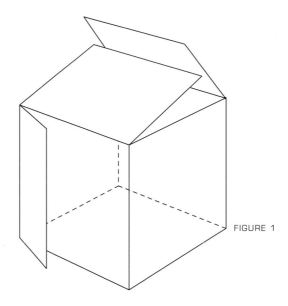

FIGURE 1

light shower parasol

TINY LIGHTS TWINKLE LIKE glistening raindrops through this luminous paper parasol. Placed on the ground in the garden or grouped and hung from the ceiling, paper parasols add a romantic, exotic touch to any event. Like all paper objects used with lights, the parasols are fragile, so keep them protected from rain and sprinklers, and tuck them in a corner away from playful pets.

WHAT YOU NEED

Paper parasol
1 strand of 100 clear mini-lights
Floral tape
Floral wire
Extension cord
Scissors
Hot-glue gun and glue sticks
Low-tack masking tape

INSTRUCTIONS

1. Open the parasol. If you are superstitious, you might want to work on this project outside! Position the plug end of the mini-light strand at the end of the handle. Use the floral tape to secure the cord along the handle in several places.

2. Unwind a length of floral wire and cut it into several 4-inch (10 cm) lengths. Set the lengths of wire aside.

3. Place the parasol upside down on the floor or on a table. This makes it easy to rotate the umbrella as you position the light strand.

4. Wind the light strand around the stretcher of the parasol, fastening it with short lengths of wire. Give each wire a few twists to secure the strand.

5. When you have finished wiring the strand to the stretcher, spiral the rest of the strand out toward the edge of the parasol.

6. Use hot glue to attach the mini-light strand to the ribs. Small strips of low-tack masking tape help position the strand on the parasol. Use the tape to hold the strand in place on either side of the rib where you plan to glue it. Leave the strips of tape in place until the glue has thoroughly cooled. Remove the strips.

7. Place the completed parasol in the garden, tucked behind low-growing plants or by the front entrance of your home.

summer night parties

Summer means longer, warmer evenings and casual gatherings outside where you have space enough to be exuberant and time to tell stories late into the night. Many of the mini-light projects in other sections of the book can be adapted for summertime fun. Here are a few meant especially for those special nights.

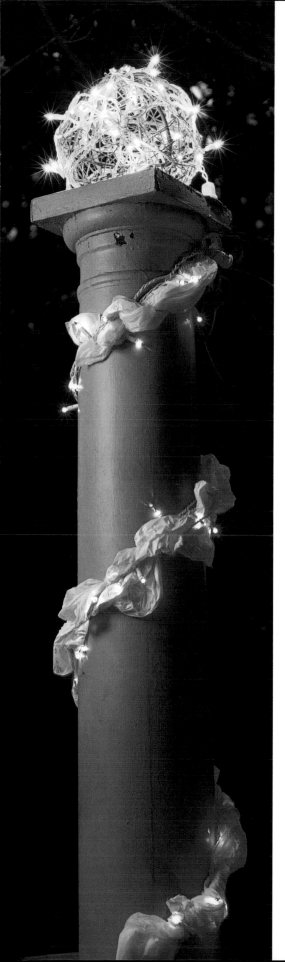

SALVAGED ARCHITECTURAL PIECES ARE POPULAR decorating elements. Used judiciously they can fit into just about any environment. But they don't usually have a sense of humor—something we think is absolutely essential for a proper summer party! We thought going gaudy would be totally glorious. So we dressed up two charming old columns with trash bags (you heard right!) and lots of lights and transformed an ordinary summer deck into the neighborhood conversation piece. Hey, if you're going to decorate like this, you're not going to be able to keep your party a secret, so just go ahead and invite everybody!

stupendous salvaged columns

WHAT YOU NEED

White plastic trash bags
2 strands of purple lights on white cord
2 strands of gold lights on green cord
2 grapevine balls to match the size of the columns

INSTRUCTIONS

1   To add dimension to the columns, first knot and twist several ordinary white plastic bags together to make a single strand about 5 feet (1.5 m) long. Wrap the purple lights and the plastic together around the columns. Four twists around the column is enough—you don't want to hide the texture of the column. Attach the combination to the column with thumbtacks.

2. Next, wrap gold lights around the grapevine balls, and attach the balls to the top of the columns with thumbtacks.

3. Run all the cords down the back sides of the columns.

We know it—you're going to say, "Hey, this looks more shabby than 'shabby chic!'" That's true, but only during the flat light of day. At night, when darkness creates a theatrical backdrop and the lights glitter unabashedly, it all looks positively wonderful.

tomato cage chandelier

TURN AN ORDINARY WIRE TOMATO cage upside down, trim it, twist it, curl up its edges, festoon it with mini-lights and gaudy ornaments, and hang it up high for all the world to see. You've made a chandelier even the Phantom of the Opera would envy!

We used clear lights and shiny gold ornaments to play up our faux retro-glamour look. You can get completely different yet equally fun looks with blue lights and rhinestone bracelets or green lights with pink flamingo ornaments. Or how about going all out—attach a blinker to the lights and watch what happens!

WHAT YOU NEED

Pyramid tomato cage

Wire cutters

Pliers

White tape

Rolling pin

Chain, cut or wrapped to the length needed

Hanging hook, if needed

Strand of 50 clear mini-lights on white cord

Ornaments

Extension cord

INSTRUCTIONS

1. With the wire cutters, cut off the top and bottom sections of the tomato cage. Using the rolling pin, bend the remaining wires back on themselves to make a decorative curve on both the top and bottom, as shown in the photo.

2. Start stringing the lights on the ribs of the cage from the bottom of it, with the unplugged end, so the plug end is at the top. Secure the lights with bits of scrap wire.

3. Cut a length of chain to connect the tomato cage to the branch of a tree. If you don't have a nearby tree, attach a hook to the ceiling and connect one end of the chain to it. Attach the other end to the top of the tomato cage and hang up the chandelier. Add the extension cord to the strand of lights and wrap it around the tree branch and down the trunk of the tree. Use thumbtacks to lightly secure it to the tree. If you're hanging the chandelier from a ceiling or deck beam, just tack the wire up gracefully, making it as inconspicuous as possible.

4. Hang ornaments from the curled tips of the tomato cage.

5. Give the whole thing a whirl for good luck.

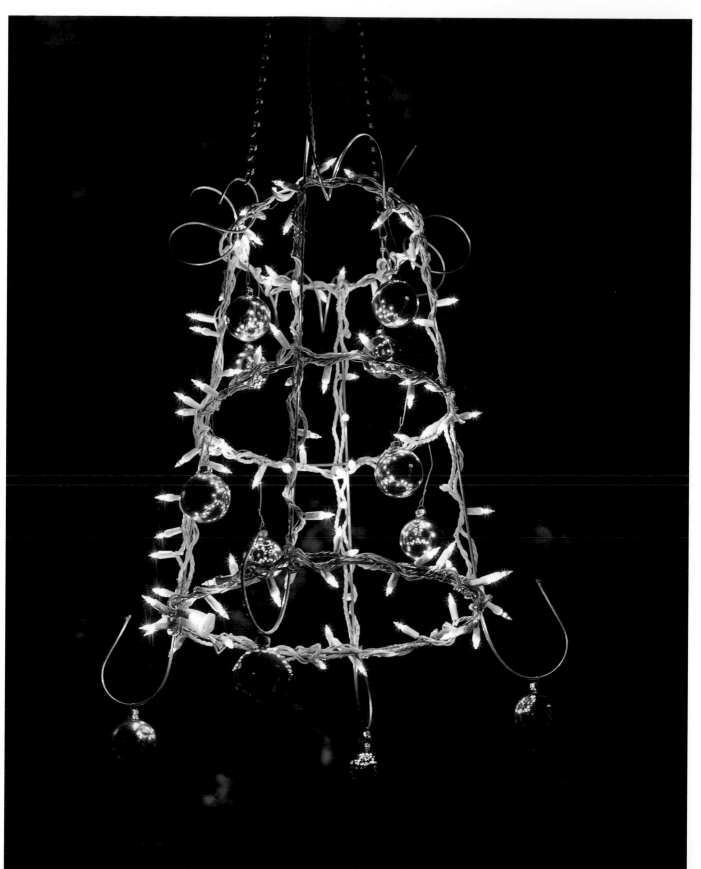

tubs of lights
and beer

BIG, BRIGHT, AND FULL OF BEER—
could there be a more perfect light display for a summer night party? An
arrangement of galvanized tubs lit by
mini-lights is a quick and easy way to
create temporary lighting in the garden.
The tubs serve a utilitarian purpose by
helping you direct party traffic to designated areas, as well as an aesthetic func-
tion by providing a dramatic uplighting
effect for certain areas of landscaping.
Galvanized tubs come in all sizes and
shapes, so you can mix and match, and
scatter them all gaily throughout the
garden. And if it rains? Seems like a perfectly good excuse to bring the tubs indoors—maybe for the rest of the year!

All we did was arrange different-size
tubs and put lots of mini-lights in them.
For the beer tub, of course you don't
want to put the lights next to the ice, so
we filled a small bucket with lights and
squeezed it into the ice. It lit up the beer
like a beacon. Gives new meaning to
"lite" beer, don't you think?

night-wishes light shades

EVERY EVENING IS A NIGHT TO
remember with these twinkling night-sky
light shades made out of cookie cutters and
waxed paper. It's is a perfect project to make
with children. They love cutting out the
shapes and shaving their crayons to get the
color on the waxed paper. Little imperfections
only add to the design's charm. When the
party is over, hang the lights in the child's
room and make secret wishes.

WHAT YOU NEED

1 strand of 50 clear mini-lights

Cookie cutters, as many as needed for your
    string of lights

Rubber vacuum cleaner belt, ¾ inch (1.9 cm) wide

Waxed paper

Craft paper

Wax crayons

Metal snips or very sharp scissors

Craft knife

Hot-glue gun and glue sticks

Handheld pencil sharpener

Iron

Felt-tip pen

INSTRUCTIONS

preparing the cookie cutter frames

1. From the cutting edge of the cookie cutter, use metal snips to cut a square hole just large enough to thread a mini-light through. Center the hole in the side of the cutter.

2. Cut the vacuum cleaner belt into approximately ¾-inch (1.9 cm) pieces.

3. Cut a ½-inch (1.3 cm) "X" in the center of each belt section with the craft knife.

4. Hot glue the vacuum cleaner belt pieces to the inside of the cookie cutter openings, centering the "X" in the opening you made.

preparing the waxed paper covers

5. Cut the waxed paper into a 12 x 24-inch (30 x 61.5 cm) sheet.

6. Fold and crease the waxed paper sheet in half, then open it out flat on a piece of craft paper. Over one half of the waxed paper, shave the crayons with a handheld pencil sharpener, scattering the shavings over the waxed paper. Repeat with a second color.

7. Fold the clean half of the waxed paper sheet over the half with the shavings, then cover it with two sheets of craft paper.

8. With the iron set at a medium temperature (no steam), press the iron onto the sandwiched paper and shavings. Pull back the craft paper and check your progress after every second pass with the iron. Stop ironing when the crayon shavings have melted.

9. Let the waxed paper cool for approximately five minutes.

10. Repeat with the other pairs of color combinations, creating differently colored covers for each shape of cookie cutter (three different color combinations were used for the pictured lights).

assembling the cookie-cutter lights

11. Place the cookie cutters on top of the finished waxed paper sheets; trace the cookie cutters onto the colored waxed paper with a felt-tip pen, then flip over the cookie cutter and trace out the other side (each cookie cutter needs two covers).

12. Cut out the traced shapes with a craft knife.

13. Hot glue the edges of the cut-out shapes to the cookie cutters.

14. Insert a light into the openings that were cut in the cookie cutters.

patio umbrella with light rays

EVEN IN DAYLIGHT, MINI-LIGHTS CAN be seen in the shaded underside of a patio umbrella, sparkling the whole dining area. At night, the lights shine much more clearly, giving a warm "Let's stay here forever" feeling to the evening.

The trick to lighting table umbrellas is to avoid placing the lights on the pole. You don't want the lights to glare in people's eyes while they're trying to talk to one another. The easiest way to do this is to buy mini-light sets designed specifically for use on patio umbrellas. But if you didn't plan far enough ahead to do that, here are some tips to do the job with ordinary strings of mini-lights.

If you're lucky enough to have a column nearby, such as the one in the photograph, then make things easy on yourself and use it as a handy place to start stringing your lights, working your way down it to the tips of the open umbrella. In this way you can avoid setting lights on the umbrella pole. If you don't have a column nearby, a fence or tree branch would do. Even more spectacular would be to make a Twinkling Trellis (see page 63) and use it as a companion to the dining set.

If your table has no upright structure on which to start the lights, then you'll have to bring your string of lights up from the pole. The easiest thing to do is to run extension cords up the pole first, so there are no lights on the pole, and start the light bulbs in the umbrella itself.

Or you could disguise the lights on the pole. A lovely way to do that is to wind the lights through a garland of flowers and seashells. But unlike other garlands, such as the Little Princess Canopy on page 29, where the lights are intended to be seen, you could tweak the lights into the petals and leaves on the pole, so they show less.

If you're going to be gentle when you open and close your umbrella, (meaning you're not going to assign the task to a teenager!) or if the weather in your area allows you to leave the umbrella open safely all season, then just use floral tape to attach the lights. Otherwise, take the extra precaution of using wire to keep the lights securely wound around the umbrella ribs.

Match the lights to your umbrella. Clear lights are always a safe and classy choice, but feel free to experiment with colors, especially the new strands of lights that come with beautiful combinations of colors already chosen for you.

AN ALTERNATIVE TO LIGHTING THE RIBS OF A PATIO UMBRELLA IS TO TAKE THE LAZY SUMMER PARTYGIVER'S WAY OUT—AND JUST HANG COLORED LIGHT BALLS FROM THE EDGES OF THE UMBRELLA.

autumn outdoors

Leaves are falling. It's time for plaids and woolens, for family gatherings to give thanks for nature's bounty, and to cheer together for our favorite teams. Many of the projects in this book are suitable for autumn events if you use fall colors such as burnt orange, oak leaf red, amber, and gold. With the cooler temperatures, most occasions for mini-lights are indoors. Except Halloween, the night when goblins rule and the timid better be wary!

halloween house

IT'S GUARANTEED YOU'LL GET ALL THE trick-or-treaters at your place on fright-night if you create a sparkling bat-windowed Spook Haven. We did it with an old potting shed, complete with a real creaking off-the-hinges door, but you can follow the same theme for a whole house. We added a touch of the Gothic with another project, a lighted metal topiary ball.

We used outdoor icicle lights, the same kind that are so popular for winter lighting—in orange—and strings of orange lights, also designed for outdoor use. In case you were expecting fancy guests (Count Dracula, perhaps?) you could exchange some of the orange bulbs with gold and give the ghouls a touch of glitter. Depending on the weather, and how long you want the lights to stay up, attach the cords with mini-light clips, hooks, nails, or thumbtacks.

To give dimension to the windows, we covered them with strips of purple cellophane, which contrasted eerily with the orange lights. To make the bats, we drew bat shapes on black construction paper, cut them out, and taped them to the window. You could also create ghosts or fang-toothed monsters in the same way. You'll have no trouble finding Halloween-themed lights—manufacturers love coming up with all kinds of creepy-crawly light forms and shades. Would you like a giant jack-o-lantern? Or how about skeletons on string or a huge spider?

When doing such a large installation, it's essential that you take the time to plan. Measure how much of the structure you want to cover with your lights and match it to the light lengths of the cords, which are listed on the package of the lights. Factor in the length of the cords' unlighted leads so you don't have any gaps in the coverage. Always have more lights than you think you'll need, just in case.

Except for the fact that we had to climb up and down the ladder to hang the lights from the eaves, the whole project was really easy. The hard part was trying not to eat all the Halloween candy!

great balls of fire topiary

THIS TOPIARY ADDS A TOUCH OF HUMOR to the Halloween House, but in a different setting, it can be an elegant and versatile garden accent. Choose bulb colors that reflect the time of year: orange for autumn, white for winter, green for spring, or red for summer. Create a pair to flank a walkway or stand sentinel in a night garden.

The topiary form can be placed directly in the ground but you may need to steady it with a stone or brick. For a more permanent installation, anchor the form in a decorative terra-cotta pot filled with soil and planted with annuals.

Floral tape is a great aid to wrapping strands of lights around topiaries and other garden structures. Especially on round shapes with many sections like this project, you'll use lots of tape.

WHAT YOU NEED

Wire globe topiary form
1 or 2 strands of mini-lights
Floral tape
Extension cord

INSTRUCTIONS

1. Decide the best arrangement for the mini-lights before starting to place them on the topiary form. Consider how tightly you want to string the lights and determine whether or not you need more than one strand.

2. Wind the plug end of the mini-light strand up the base of the form, using the floral tape to secure it.

3. Place the lights evenly around the ball, securing the strand with floral tape. To keep the lights evenly spaced, you may need to change the direction in which you wind the mini-light strand. If so, use the floral tape to reinforce the strand in the places you change directions.

4. Plug the strand into an extension cord. If you want to camouflage it, wrap it with the floral tape.

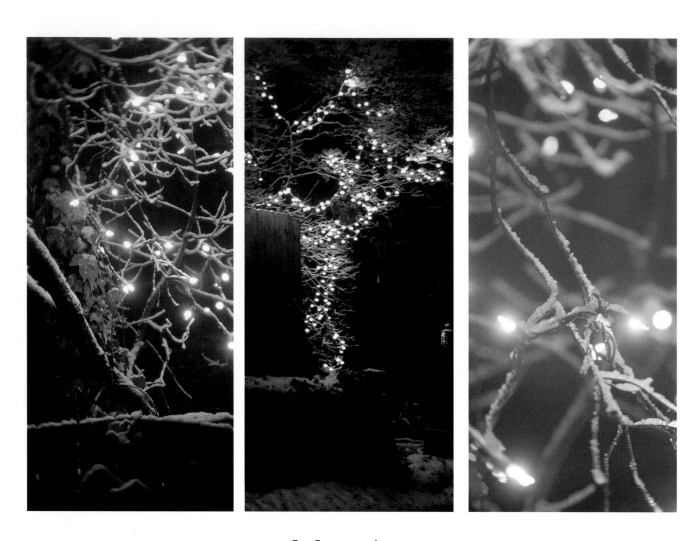

celebrating winter

Mini-lights were made for winter. They grew out of the tradition of Christmas lighting and came into their own as people demanded easier, more reliable ways to add sparkle to their homes. Although mini-lights are used year round now, they remain most popular during the winter holidays. Here are some projects that celebrate winter and the events that make it our most festive season.

A TUTEUR, FROM THE FRENCH word for trainer (as in training climbing plants), is a trellis in the shape of an obelisk. In a summer garden, this magnificent tuteur would be covered with vibrant flowers, such as roses and clematis or the delicate tendrils of peas and beans. As this photo shows, with the addition of mini-lights, these useful garden structures can be transformed into glittering sculptures that celebrate the special beauty of winter.

Indoors, an array like this would be a spectacular holiday tree. Instead of using a snow-filled tub, set it on the floor and surround it with pinecones and gift-wrapped presents.

Arrange the mini-lights on a tuteur to suit its particular shape. With this tuteur, for example, you'd want to show off its lovely shape by spiraling the lights loosely up the long center, and then bunching them more effusively at the top to accentuate its crowning glory. With a more simple tuteur, embellish it with colored lights, or cluster lights such as those in the shapes of grapes or berries. To hold the light strands in place, use strips of wire to match the color of the metal in the structure.

glowing snowballs centerpiece

SNOWBALL-SHADED MINI-LIGHTS, JUST the size of holiday tree ornaments, are perfect for winter table arrangements. Choose a container that is raised slightly, such as a cake stand or compote bowl, or as we did, a dessert bowl with feet. The pearly translucent luster of milk glass is especially lovely in wintry displays.

When using a lush arrangement such as this one, keep your table settings and linens simple. White is always beautiful and reflects more of the lights, but any solid color tablecloth would look attractive.

Pick nice fresh greens. We used ivy, but evergreens would be beautiful, too. Clean off any dirt and dry the greens thoroughly before placing them on the table. Weave a strand of 10 snowball lights through the ivy, wind it into a loose circle, and place it into the bowl. Let the plug end of the cord lead hang down the side of the table. Clip the

cord to the table with sturdy bull dog clips, the kind used to hold big manuscripts. Add a few shiny colored ball ornaments to the bowl. Then add another branch of ivy to cascade down the side of the bowl that will face the center of the table.

Depending on the size of your table, weave a garland of clear mini-lights on green cord through another few branches of ivy, tucking the plug end under the bowl so it goes down the table and out of sight. Then tuck the garland under the branch trailing from the bowl so it looks like one continuous path of ivy. Attach red and silver ornaments with floral wire. Vary the look by combining large ornaments with tiny ones of the same or complementary colors.

This arrangement looks festive on a mantle or outside on a bench near the front door to welcome guests. Make two to brighten up both ends of a buffet table.

vintage
holiday bulb
display

THIS JAPANESE LANTERN BULB DATES
FROM THE 1910s. THE FIRST HOLIDAY
LIGHTS ON A STRING WERE MANUFACTURED
IN THE U.S. IN 1903.

VINTAGE HOLIDAY BULBS SEEM TO GET LOST
when combined with contemporary decorations. We felt these
beautiful old lights deserved a display all their own. Whether you
use old or new lights, this simple design is suitable for apartments,
offices, and other places where space for holiday decorations may
be scarce.

We wanted to make the display frame out of a tall, simple structure that wouldn't compete with the bulbs and would provide
ample space to show them off. We found such a frame in the mini-
malist lines of steel concrete reinforcement grids, which are sold
in home improvement centers. Then we loosely trailed each
strand up the grid, securing them with wire.

Keep your eye out for loose bulbs in tag sales and thrift shops.
Eventually you'll have enough to combine them into a display.
And don't worry if you're missing a bulb on a strand of lights.
If you're as old as the vintage bulbs, you might be missing a few
parts, too, so just let the old bulbs be honored as they are! It's all
part of their charm.

THESE BULBS WERE IN USE FROM THE 1920s TO 1940s.

cane
cone shades

ELEGANT, STURDY, AND EASY TO make, these mini-light shades provide a distinctive look we've seen nowhere else. The stiff ice-cream cone shape is machine-made caning, the same material that comes from the outer skin of the rattan vine and is used to make cane chair seats. Sheets of machine-made caning come in many different weaves. You can find them through handicraft suppliers and furniture refinishers. If you handle the cones carefully and pack them with tissue paper, these shades can last for years.

WHAT YOU NEED

Sheets of pre-woven chair caning,
   cut into 4-inch (10 cm) squares
Scissors
White acrylic spray paint (optional)
Strong adhesive glue
Clamps

INSTRUCTIONS

1. Determine how many shades you'll want for your arrangement. Cut out a 4-inch (10 cm) square of fabric for each light.

2. The cane naturally is a lovely pale beige color, which would look wonderful on wood tabletops in rustic decors. If you want the snowy look seen in the photo, spray-paint the caning with white acrylic paint. Let it dry thoroughly.

3. Roll the square into a cone, leaving a tiny hole just big enough to thread the strand of lights through the bottom of the cone. Secure the sides closed with strong adhesive glue, and use clamps to hold the sides together until the glue is thoroughly dry.

4. Fringe the outer edge by cutting off a few of the cross canes.

5. For a more glamorous look, spray the cones gold, or mix white and gold cones in an arrangement. Caning doesn't look its best in dark intense colors, so if you want to color it, stick with the pale tones.

ONE OF THE EASIEST WAYS TO SPARKLE a room for a party is to decorate the tables, and the easiest tables to decorate are round ones. So if you have a choice, go round. In addition to string lights, we used a set of hedge lights—the kind used outdoors to sparkle your shrubbery. It's already woven to a round shape and easy to hang.

One simple design trick can make all the difference with a decorated table. Make pedestals of different heights underneath the fabric to give a variety of elevations to the items displayed on the table. Pedestals? Hey, it's painless. We just used books from the pile waiting to be returned to the library! It's as easy as that.

Once you make your first decorated table, be warned: your friends will be calling on you all the time to "do this one little table for me, won't you?" You don't have to tell them how easy it is! But do be on the lookout for pieces of interesting fabric, especially shiny and sheer pieces that you can add to your table decorating supplies.

These directions are for a standard 36-inch (91 cm) round table. Modify them for larger tables.

dazzling dessert table

WHAT YOU NEED

Blue satin tablecloth to fit your table

1½ yards (1.38 m) of blue velour

4 yards (3.6 m) of shiny sheer white fabric

4 yards (3.6 m) of blue tulle

1 set of hedge lights

1 strand of clear mini-lights on white cord

1 strand of blue mini-lights on white cord

T-pins

Pile of sturdy hardback books

1 . Plan out ahead of time how you'll want your desserts and dishes arranged on the table so you'll know the heights you want to make the platforms.

2 . Cover the table with a blue satin tablecloth.

3 . With the T-pins, attach a set of hedge lights around the sides of the table, starting at the rim of the table and working your way down, as if you're tacking a skirt around the table.

4 . Stack the books to make different heights for your pedestals. Then cover everything carefully with the blue velour, fluffing it up to look nice. Lay a strand of colored white lights randomly on top of the velour. You don't have to be too precise, just make sure the plug cord hangs down the back.

5 . Then cover all this with the 4 yards (3.6 m) of the very sheer white fabric and drape it gracefully over the table.

6 . Next make a garland of tulle and lights to decorate the outside rim of the table. Lay out the tulle and place the strand of blue lights in it, then roll it up like a loose cigar, leaving the plug end hanging loose. Start at the back of the table and work your way around. Gather the garland and give it a few twists every foot (30 cm) or so, to make it look nicely bunched. Tack it onto the table with T-pins.

7 . Fluff everything up, putting in more tacks where needed, and bring on the sweets.

lighted grapevine ball

THE RUSTIC BEAUTY OF THIS festive ball comes from the combined elegance of natural materials and minimal lighting. The loveliness is compounded when you make a display with several balls, especially if you place them on a reflective surface, such as highly polished wood or a bed of crumpled gold foil.

Experiment with the strands of lights so you choose a length that is appropriate for the size ball you plan to make. For example, a small fist-size ball, such as the one in the photograph, wouldn't need a strand with more than 50 micro mini-slights. A cantaloupe-size ball might take 100 lights. If you don't have any dried berries, artificial ones in muted tones will look fine.

WHAT YOU NEED

Grapevines

1 strand of micro mini-lights on green cord, length depends on the size of the ball

Decorative sheets of moss

Floral spray paint in basil or moss color

Polystyrene foam ball

Dried berries

U-pins

INSTRUCTIONS

1. If the grapevines aren't pliable, soak them in warm water for an hour or so until they are. Dry off the surfaces.

2. Lay out the sheet of moss and fluff it up (it gets squashed in the package). The moss turns yellow over time, so to keep it green, spray it with green floral paint. (The floral paint is diluted and thus works well on fragile things like flowers and moss.) When the moss is dry, wrap it around the foam ball and secure it with U-pins.

3. Loosely wrap grapevines around the moss ball. Cut and tuck in any straggly ends.

4. Wrap lights around the ball through the grapevines, keeping the plug end where you intend the back and bottom of the ball to be. Attach berries or other natural decorations.

snow queen gazebo

GAZEBOS ARE LARGE FREESTANDING garden structures meant to provide a shady resting place and a pleasing view from all sides. Usually you see them placed on grassy hilltops surrounded by masses of colorful flowers. This spectacular metal Victorian gazebo, however, seems perfectly at home in pure-white snowy terrain. In fact, all it needs is the addition of mini-lights to look like the enchanted castle of the Snow Queen.

You'll need help lighting a gazebo, especially in cold weather. So plan on taking lots of time and a buddy or two to help hold the ladder securely and stand by with a thermos of hot coffee. Calculate your design needs carefully. How many light strands (depending on the design of your gazebo) will you need? How many extension cords and outlets? You'll want to light some gazebos, such as the room-size wooden ones, with simple strands of lights across the roof and window frames, and a strand or two down the stairs. In other structures, such as the one in the photo, you'll want the lights to accentuate space as a design element.

To gain the cascading starfall effect, start hanging the lights at the top of the gazebo, looping and bunching them up liberally as if you were piling up a rope of snowballs. Drape them more loosely along the sides and bottom. Secure the strands to the structure with wire or sturdy clips.

If the gazebo already has its own electricity source, just plug in the lights and enjoy. However, if you have to run cord to it and don't want it to show, you might consider digging a shallow trench to hold the cord. Snowfall will eventually hide it.

If you're planning to decorate the gazebo for a special event, set it up in plenty of time for weather to cooperate. Either new snow will fall to hide the tracks you've left, or you can smooth the snow with light brooms afterwards. And when the sun goes down and the lights go on, the project will look so magnificent that you'll wonder why you hadn't already made something so wonderful for summer, spring, and fall, too!

ALTHOUGH RED, GREEN, AND GOLD ARE THE
most cheery holiday colors, many people consider blue,
silver, and white to be the most sophisticated wintry
combination, reminding us of the ethereal blue glow
that moonlight casts on snow-draped landscapes. Even
if you don't have beautiful vintage country doors like
the ones in this photo, you can create a similar inviting
impression by using the same design elements: mini-
lights, sheer fabric behind glass, and the color blue.

Decorating the door is quite simple. Attach strings of
lights indoors to the window frame to create the effect
of a curtain of light. In the door in the photo, four
strings of lights were used per strip of glass panes. Cut
sheer fabric to fit the window and attach it behind the
lights. If your door isn't blue, but is a color that com-
plements blue, such as white or grey, sheer fabric in a
light blue hue would look beautiful.

For a complete and balanced look that combines shape,
color, and sparkle, don't forget to add two bright lights
on either side of the door at the bottom and a shiny
ball on the top. Instead of the big candles, make ver-
sions of the hurricane lamps in the Magic Embers
Fireplace project on page 39. If you don't have an electrical outlet on the porch, simply run cords under the
door to an outlet indoors.

For the center hanging ball, any large reflective ball
surface will do. Make an arrangement of ribbons or
artificial flowers and leaves painted blue, and glue
them to the top. Then use a long, wide blue or silver
ribbon to attach the ball above the door. If you can't
attach it directly above the door, an asymmetrical look
would be equally enchanting. Just hang the ball from a
metal shepherd's hook and place it in a planter at the
side of the door. Decorate your windows in a similar
way so they complement your door.

winter welcome door

acknowledgments

It's a measure of how much fun decorating with mini-lights is that we have so many people to thank for helping us with this book.

Most responsible for the radiant look of the book and its projects was art director Chris Bryant, followed closely by stylist Skip Wade and designer Terry Taylor. Designers Josena Aiello-Bader, Jeff Hamilton, Diana Light, and Nicole Tuggle added their special sparkle. Photographer Keith Wright put all our efforts into focus, giving them depth and glitter we barely imagined. Holding all the cords together and never coming un-wired was senior editor Deborah Morgenthal. Without our hard-working staff we'd have burned out long ago, so special thanks go to Heather Smith, Veronika Alice Gunter, Rain Newcomb, Nathalie Mornu, Hannes Charen, Theresa Gwynn, Rosemary Kast, and Pat Wald. Last on board, but no less dazzling, was proofreader Kim Catanzarite, and the gal who sparkle-wrapped it all, cover designer Barbara Zaretsky.

deep appreciation goes to each of the following

For the generous use of both their products and photos:

Gail Lunghi, Marketing Director, GKI Bethlehem www.gkibethlehem.com, photos on pages 8, 13 and 89

For the generous use of their products:

Pam Iams, Showroom Manager, Sterling, Inc., (800) 233-7052, www.sterling-inc.com

Kurt S. Adler / Santa's World, (212) 924-0900, www. Kurtadler.com

Up North Lighting, holiday division of Action Lighting, (800) 248-0076, www.upnorth-lighting.com

The Gardener's Cottage, Biltmore Village, NC

For the generous use of their photographs:

Smith & Hawken, (800) 776-3336, www.SmithandHawken.com, pages 95 and 106

Plow & Hearth, (800) 627-1712, www.plowhearth.com, page 88

Via Motif, (415) 454-8842 www.viamotif.com, page 16

For permission to photograph their gardens:

Jeff Webb, Asheville, NC

Bellevue Botanical Garden, Bellevue, WA, page __

Windy Meadow Nursery and Gardens, Ferndale, WA, www.Coco-coir.com

For their technical expertise:

Ann and Harold Outz, A Christmas House, Biltmore Village, NC (828) 274-1510

David Gunter, Kingston, TN

Jim Colwell, S. L. Bagby Co., Asheville, NC

Bertrand Thibault, President, SAPIN LUTIN, France

Najeh Rahman, President of Engineering, Minami International Corp.

contributing designers

CHRIS BRYANT takes lighting seriously. He claims never to have turned on an overhead light in his house, preferring to play with the effects of indirect lighting. And since helping to develop this book, mini-lights are newly added to his bag of lighting tricks. "Mini-lights are now either strung or bunched throughout my house and yard. I like them best to brighten up dinner parties because they don't need tending and don't blow out." Bryant is an art director for Lark Books, and says he's thankful every day to live in Asheville, North Carolina, with his partner, Skip Wade.

SKIP WADE makes a living making people and places look good. Specializing in fashion and domestics, he works in both still photography and film as a photo stylist, prop master, wardrobe manager, and location scout. He and his partner live in Asheville, North Carolina, where they're continually renovating a 1920s house. He loves good food, good wine, hiking, and puttering in the yard. He has contributed his talents to several Lark books including, *The New Book of Table Settings*, and *Decorating Porches and Decks*.

TERRY TAYLOR is an artist and designer. He's worked at Lark Books in Asheville, North Carolina, for several years in a variety of positions. His job du jour includes conceiving and executing projects for many Lark books, in addition to writing and editing his own books. Some of the most recent books he's contributed to include *Creative Outdoor Lighting*, *Salvage Style*, *Fantastic Gel Candles*, and *The Book of Wizard Craft*.

JOSENA AIELLO-BADER has been in the floral industry for 20+ years. She enjoys working with her teenage daughter, Ciara Rain McCaig, on various events, decorating just about anything, harvesting wild flowers, and gardening. In addition to designing projects for many other Lark books, Josena has also worked at the historic Biltmore Estate, as well as for the Warner Bros. motion picture, *Richie Rich*. She currently manages one of Asheville's top event shops, The Gardener's Corner, a sister shop to The Gardener's Cottage in nearby Biltmore Village. She resides in Asheville, North Carolina, with her husband, Tom.

JEFF HAMILTON is a clay artist specializing in raku, the ancient Japanese firing technique. Through his company, Raku Relics, his work appears in galleries throughout the East Coast. Jeff received his B.F.A from the University of North Carolina, Asheville, and has taught ceramics at local community colleges. Branching out from his clay specialty, Jeff made his first designer project for Lark with *Decorating with Mini-Lights*, and we know it won't be his last! Jeff lives in the Blue Ridge Mountains of North Carolina with his wife, Susan, and three spoiled cats, Myra, Ashes, and Abid.

DIANA LIGHT lives and works in the beautiful Blue Ridge Mountains of North Carolina. Her home/studio, like her life, is surround by glittering glass in hundreds of different forms, styles, and types. After earning her B.F.A. in painting and print-making at the University of North Carolina, Greenville, Diana extended her expertise to etching and painting of fine glass objects. Her art embraces life on many levels, from designs on custom mirrors and full-size glass table-tops to delicate handblown glass. She is the coauthor of Lark's *The Weekend Crafter: Etching Glass*. Contact her at Dianalight@hotmail.com.

NICOLE TUGGLE combines bookbinding and paper crafting techniques to create unique letters, fine art, and gift items. Visit her website at www.sigilation.com.

index